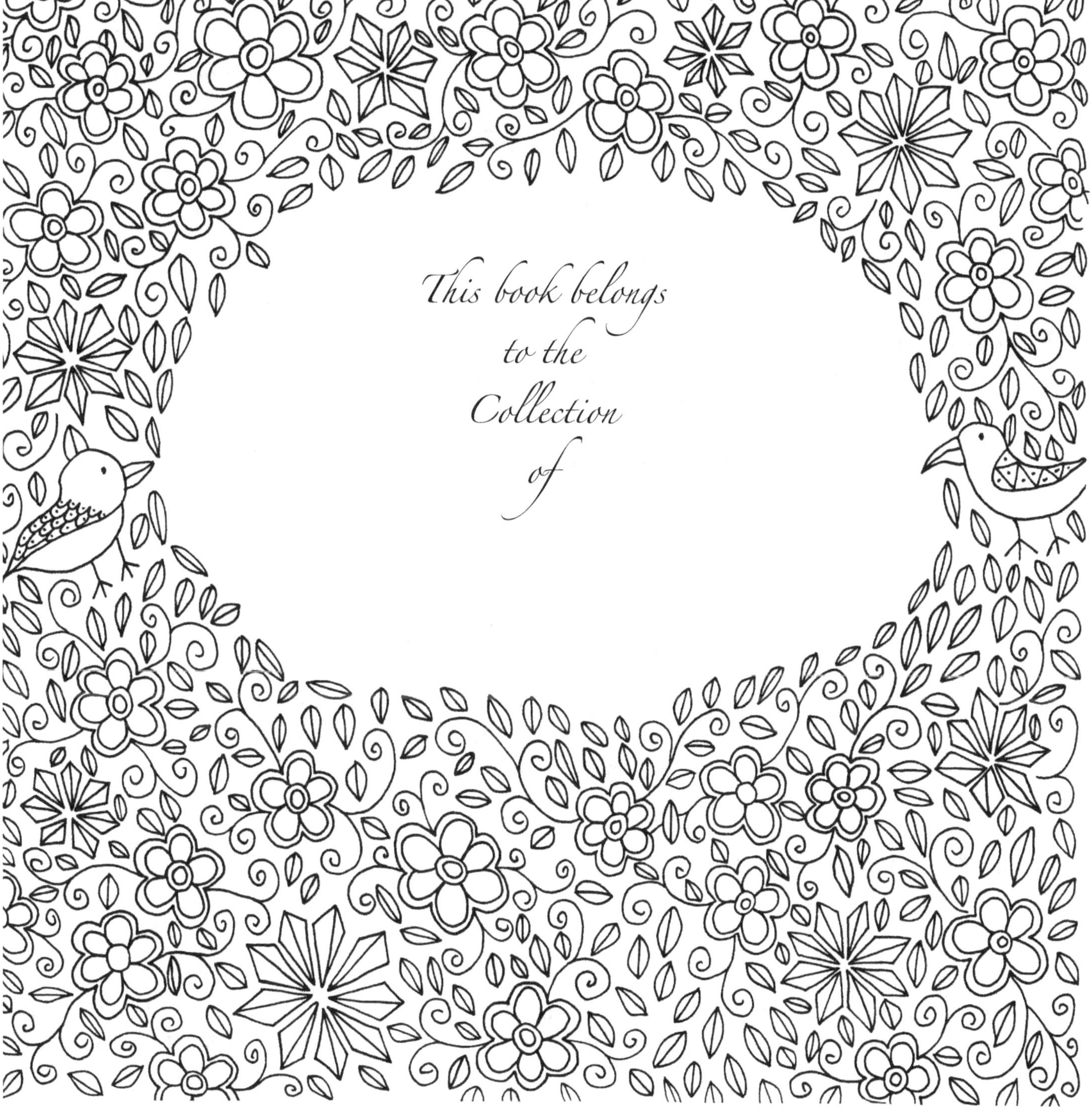

This book belongs
to the
Collection
of

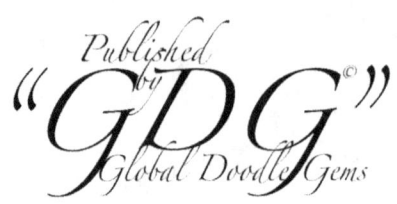

Share your colored versions with us ! We love seeing your results and hearing from you we are social !

The Official FB book page, stay on top of what we have in the works !
www.facebook.com/globaldoodlegems

The Community group, share your colored pages, meet the artists, enjoy exclusive freebies, take part in community Charity books and so much more......
www.facebook.com/groups/globaldoodlegems/

Follow us on Twitter.... @GlobalDoodlegem

We are on Instagram too
@globaldoodlegems for instagram

...and if you are not social like that we have a blog
globaldoodlegems.wordpress.com

FrontCover : Drawn & colored by Lilan Chen
BackCover : Drawn & colored by Angel Huang
Cover designed by Maria Wedel

Copyright © 2016 Global Doodle Gems

All rights are reserved by Global Doodle Gems.

Duplication of pages for personal use are allowed. You are invited to color the pages then scan/post your coloured versions to social networks, mentioning the book title and author/artist (Global Doodle Gems).

All artwork and images are protected by copyright laws. This book or any portion thereof may not, otherwise, be reproduced and/or distributed or transmitted without the express written permission of the artist/publisher of Global Doodle Gems.

All of us from the Global Doodle Gems wish you a colortastic time and look forward to seeing your wonderful color results online !

Mr. End
Lin Chiu
Damy Teng
Wenyu Lin Small Fish
Rover Hsiao
Wanting Huang
Pica Wu
Nancy 43
Lilan Chen
M. Lin
Chou Yu-Jin
Angel Huang
Happy Fishhhhhh
Leaf Yeh
Jodi Ho
Jenny Wei
Pajun Chen
Wen Kung
Hung Ai-Ling
Debbie Lai
Mina Hsiao
Jennifer Rainbow Beryllium
Kimiko Maeda
&
Jean Li

Contributing Artist
Mr. End
Taiwan

Facebook : Geometry-Flow

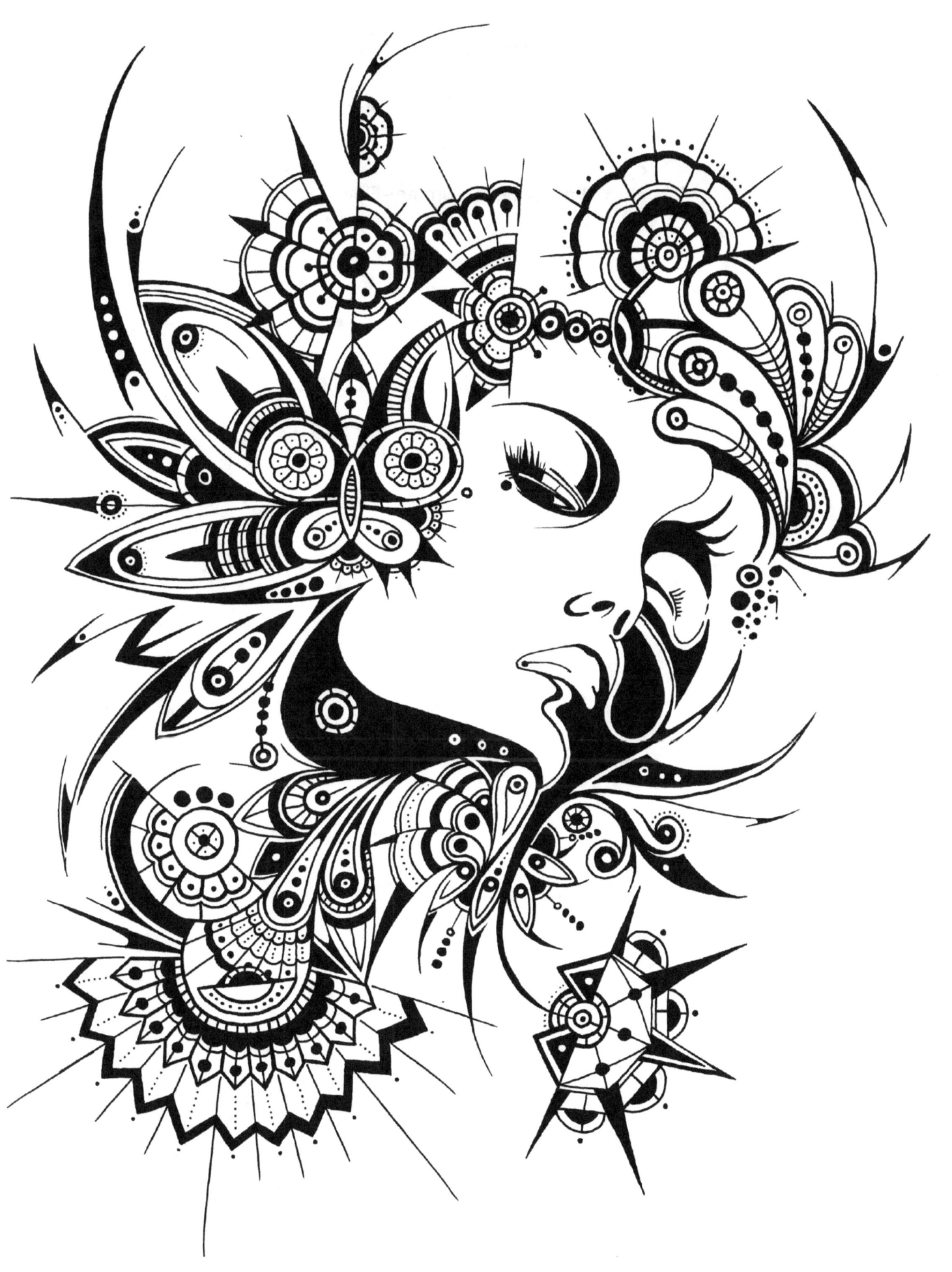

Contributing Artist
Mr. End
Taiwan

Facebook : Geometry-Flow

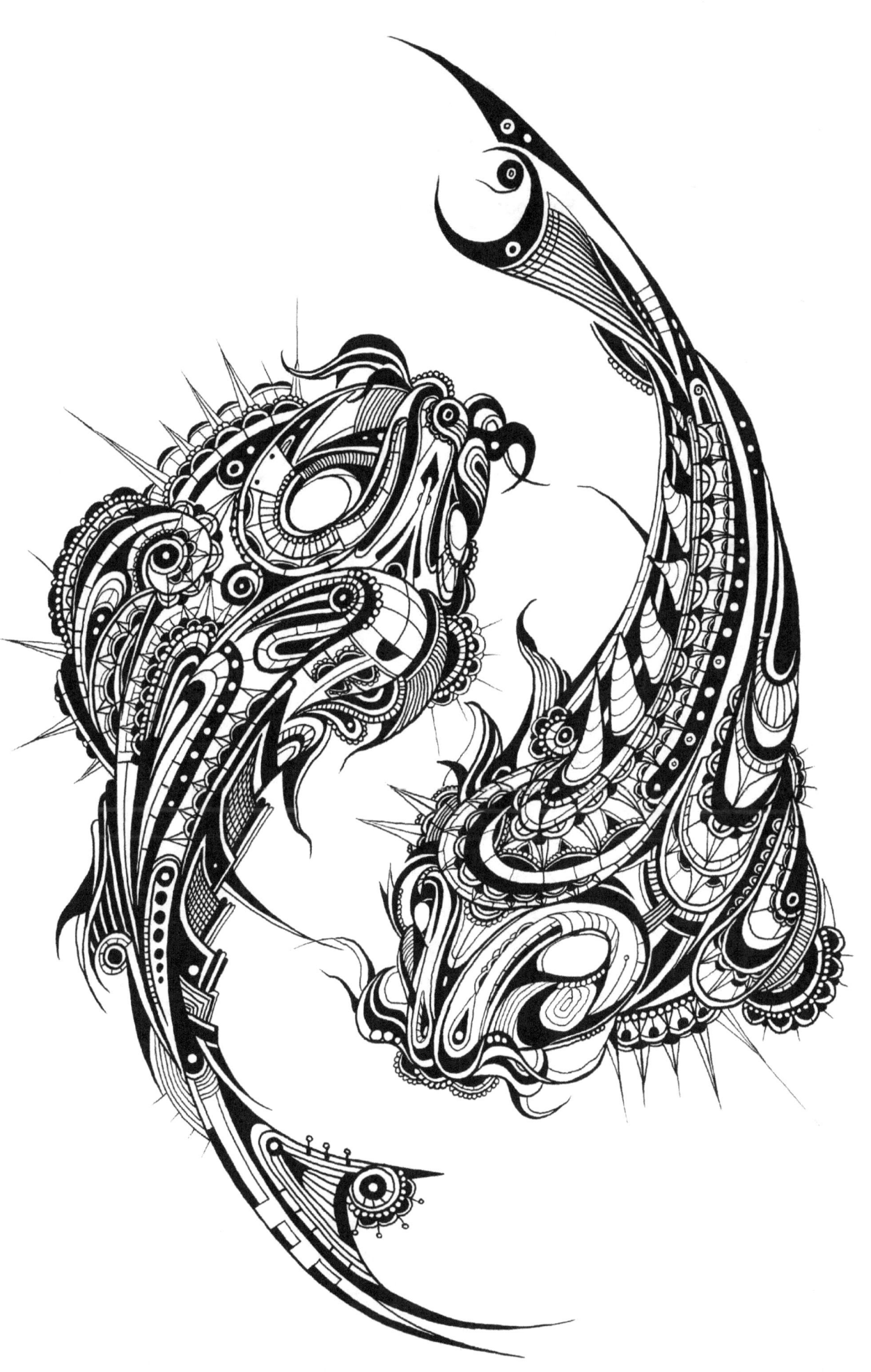

Contributing Artist
Mr. End
Taiwan

Facebook : Geometry-Flow

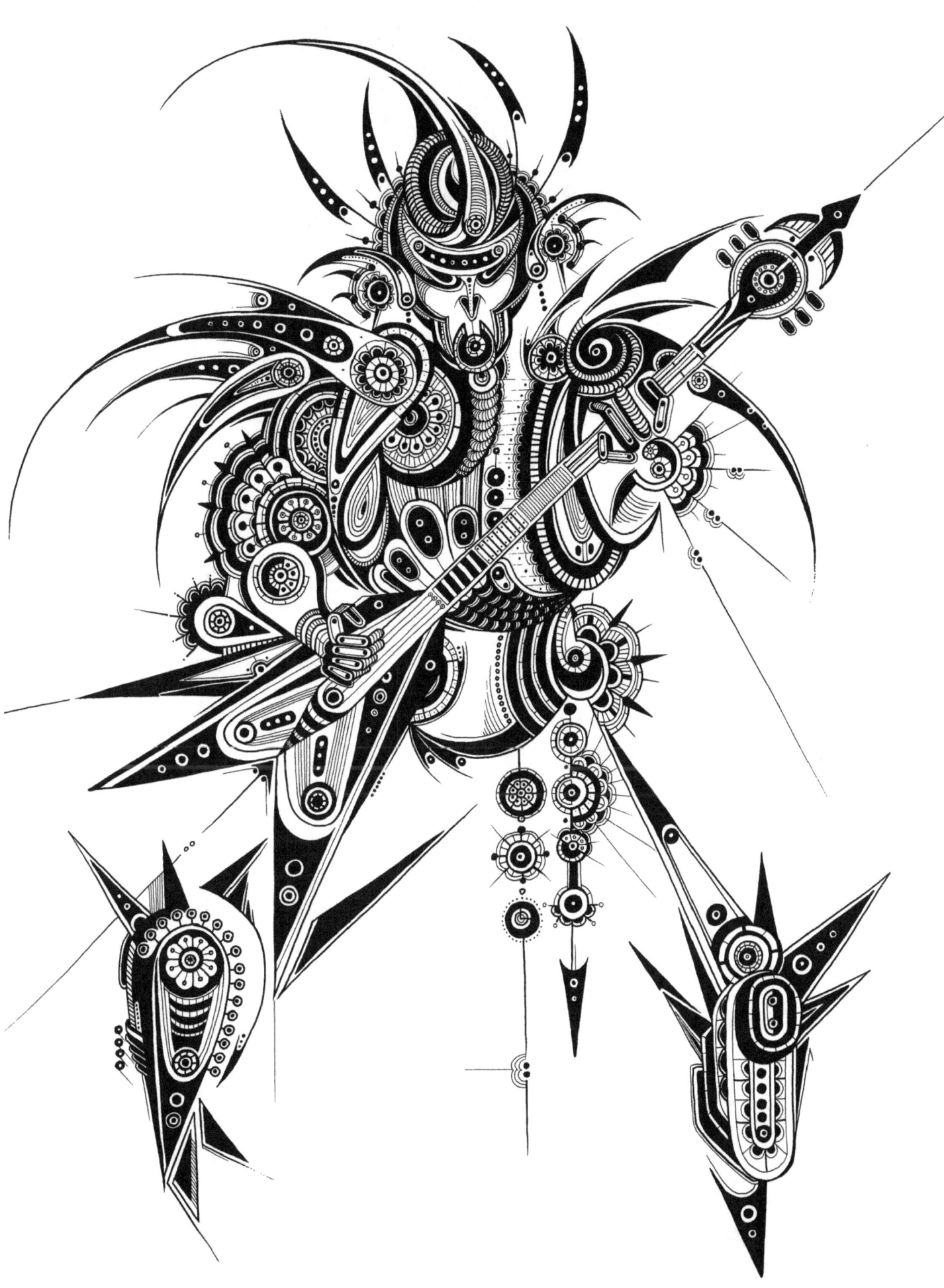

Contributing Artist
Lin Chiu
Taiwan

Facebook : ZentangleArt0626
Website : http://czt17lin.tumblr.com/

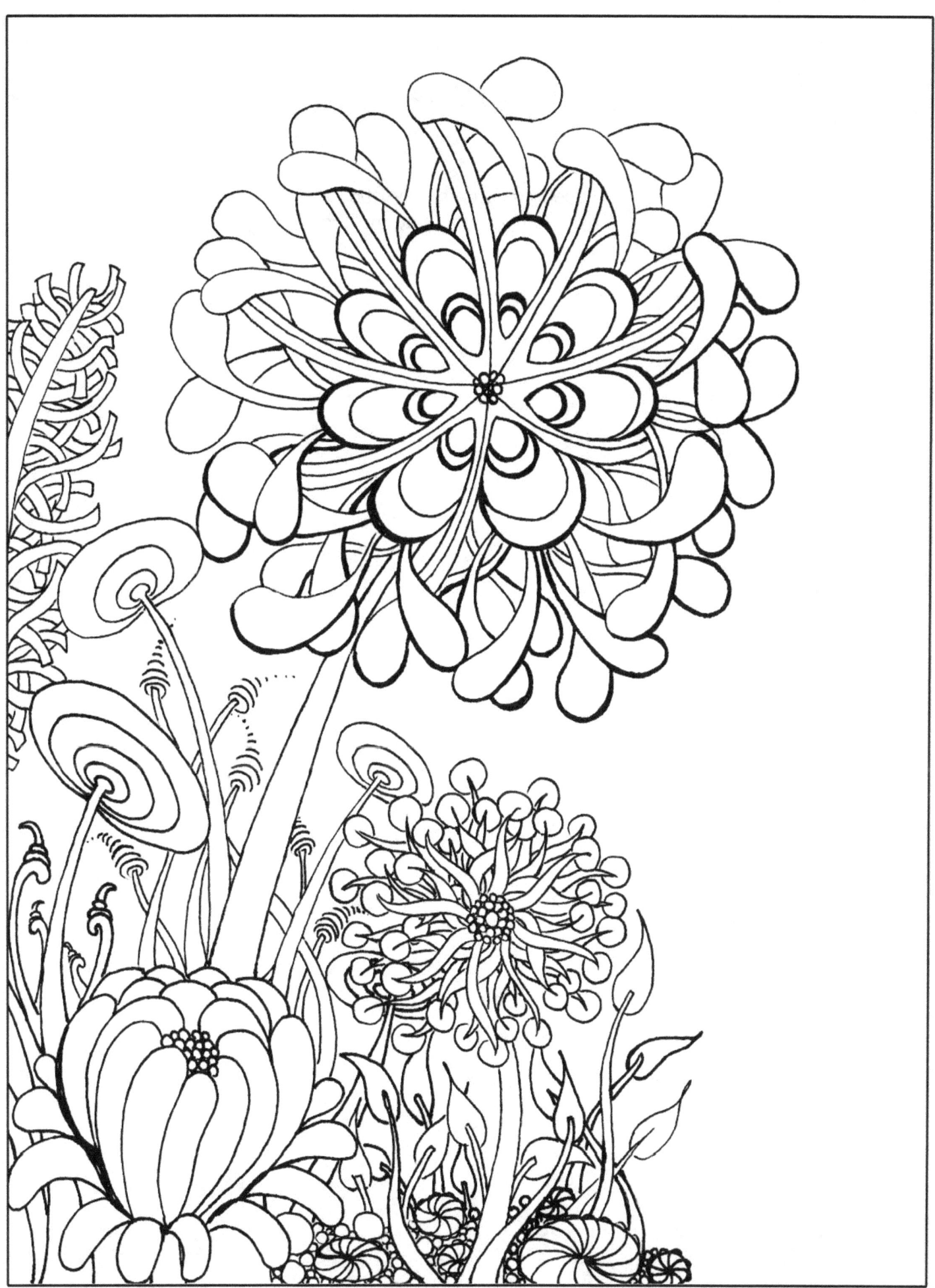

Contributing Artist
Lin Chiu
Taiwan

Facebook : ZentangleArt0626
Website : http://czt17lin.tumblr.com/

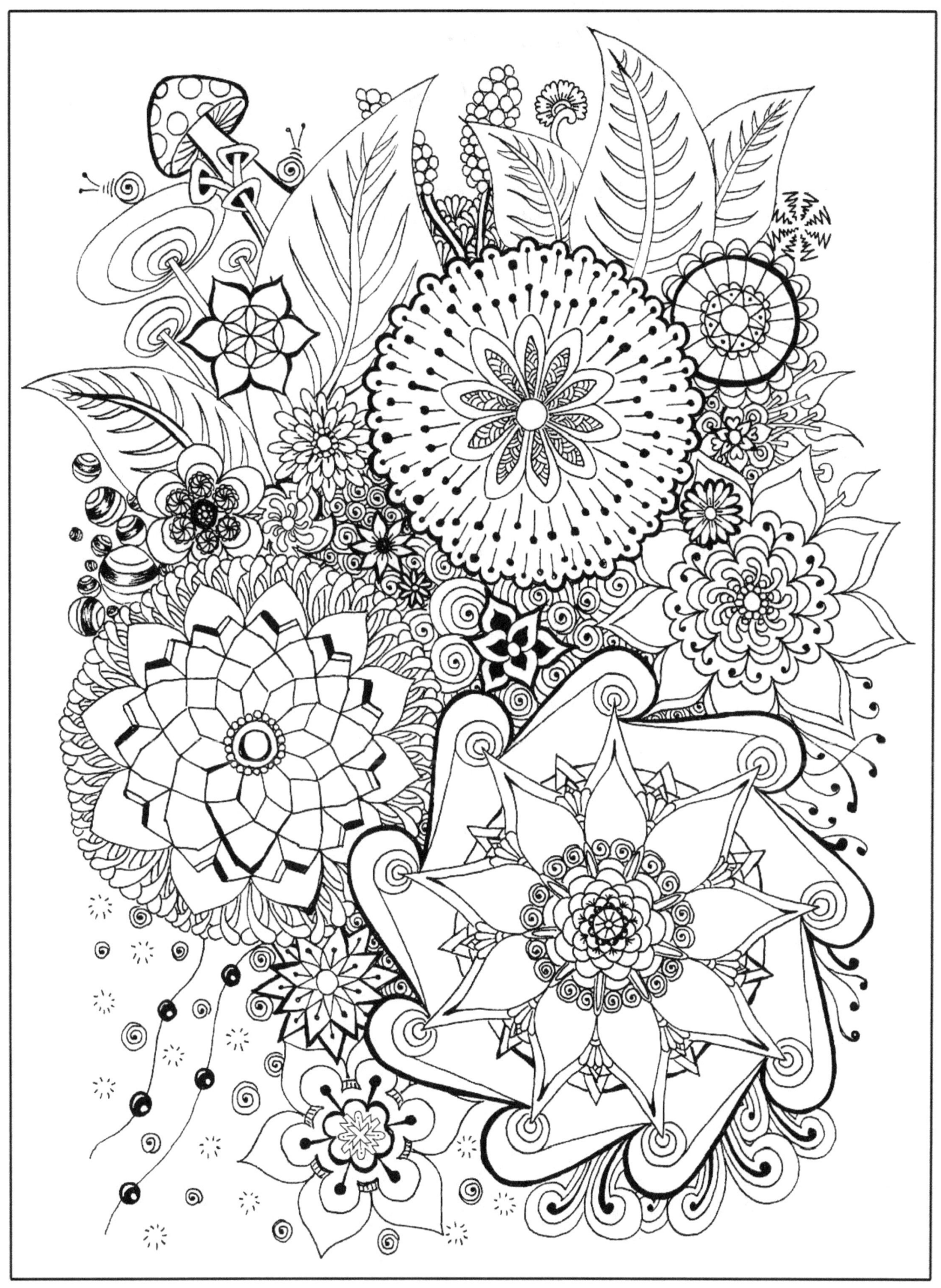

Contributing Artist
Lin Chiu
Taiwan

Facebook : ZentangleArt0626
Website : http://czt17lin.tumblr.com/

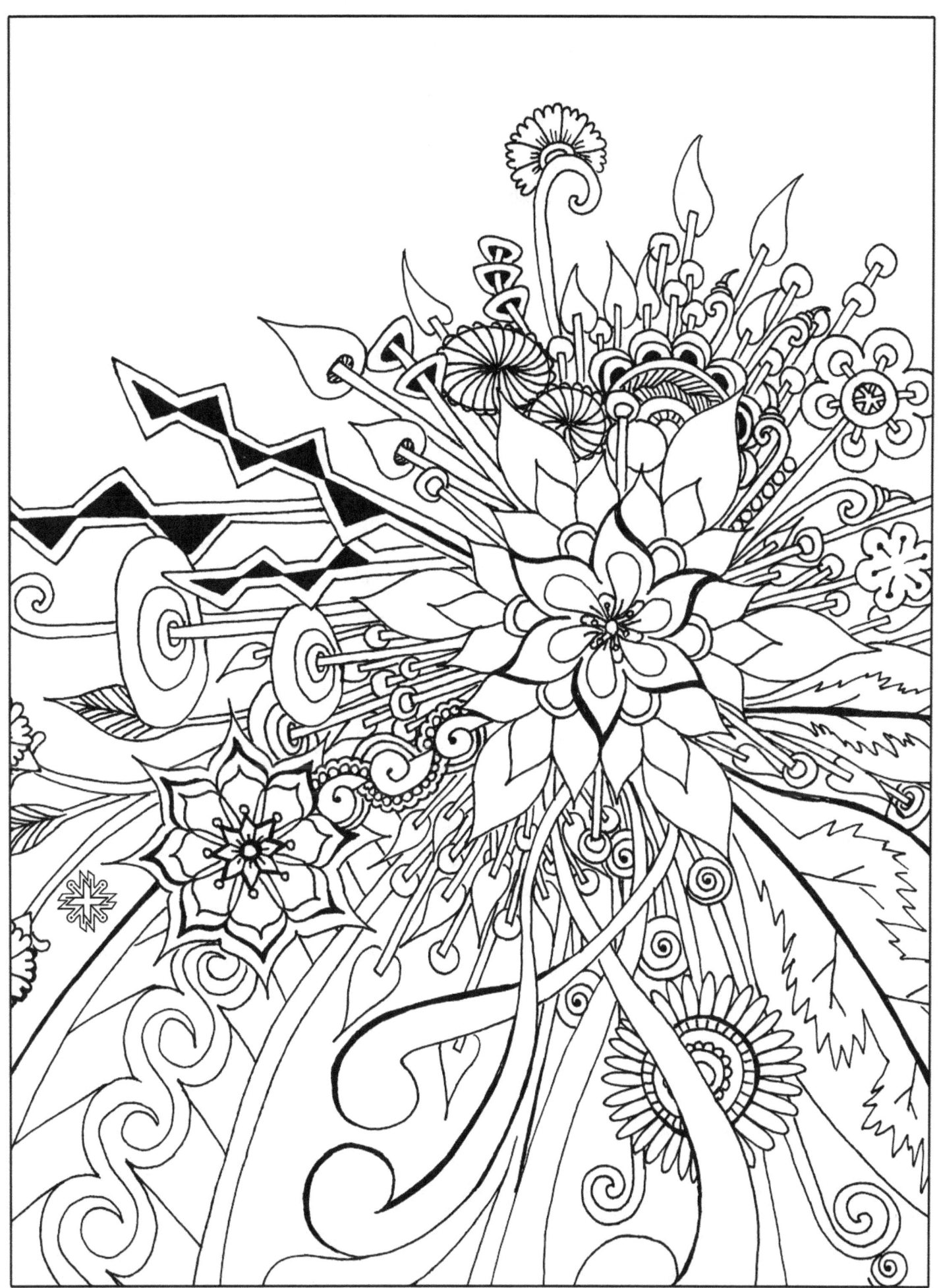

Contributing Artist
Damy Teng
Taiwan

Facebook : damy779

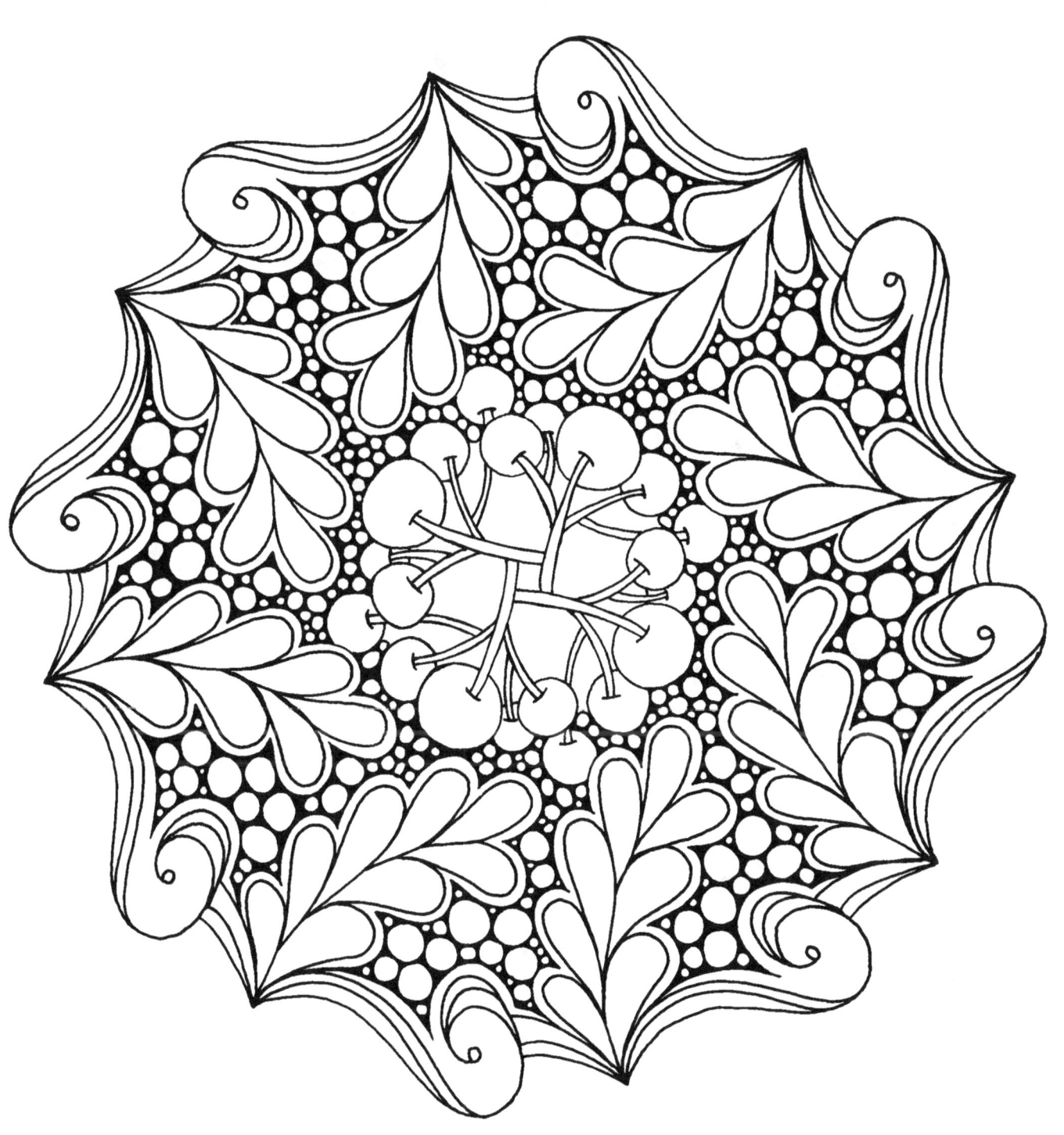

Contributing Artist
Damy Teng
Taiwan

Facebook : damy779

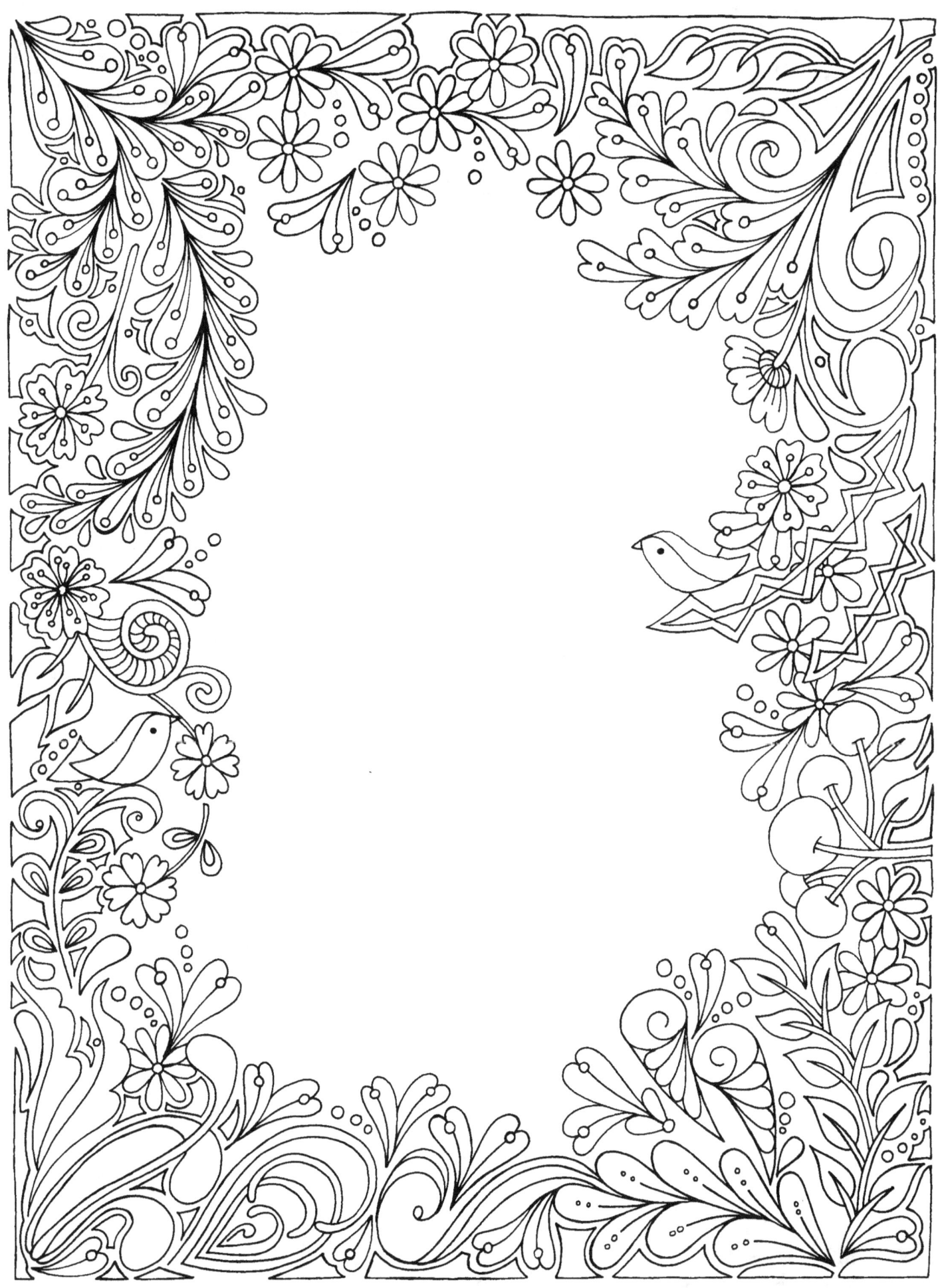

Contributing Artist
Damy Teng
Taiwan

Facebook : damy779

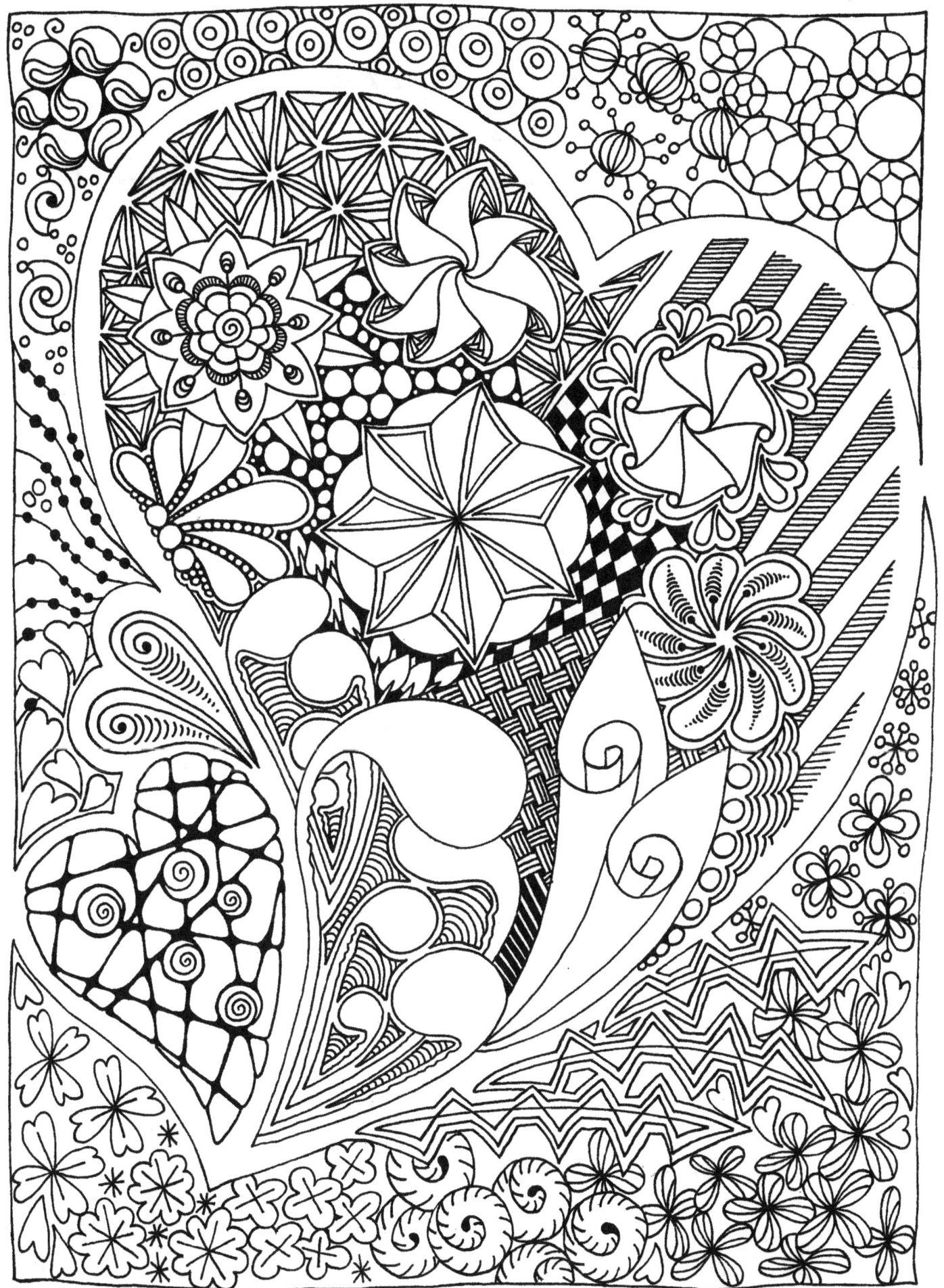

Contributing Artist
Wenyu Lin Small Fish
Taiwan

Facebook : smallfish.smallfish

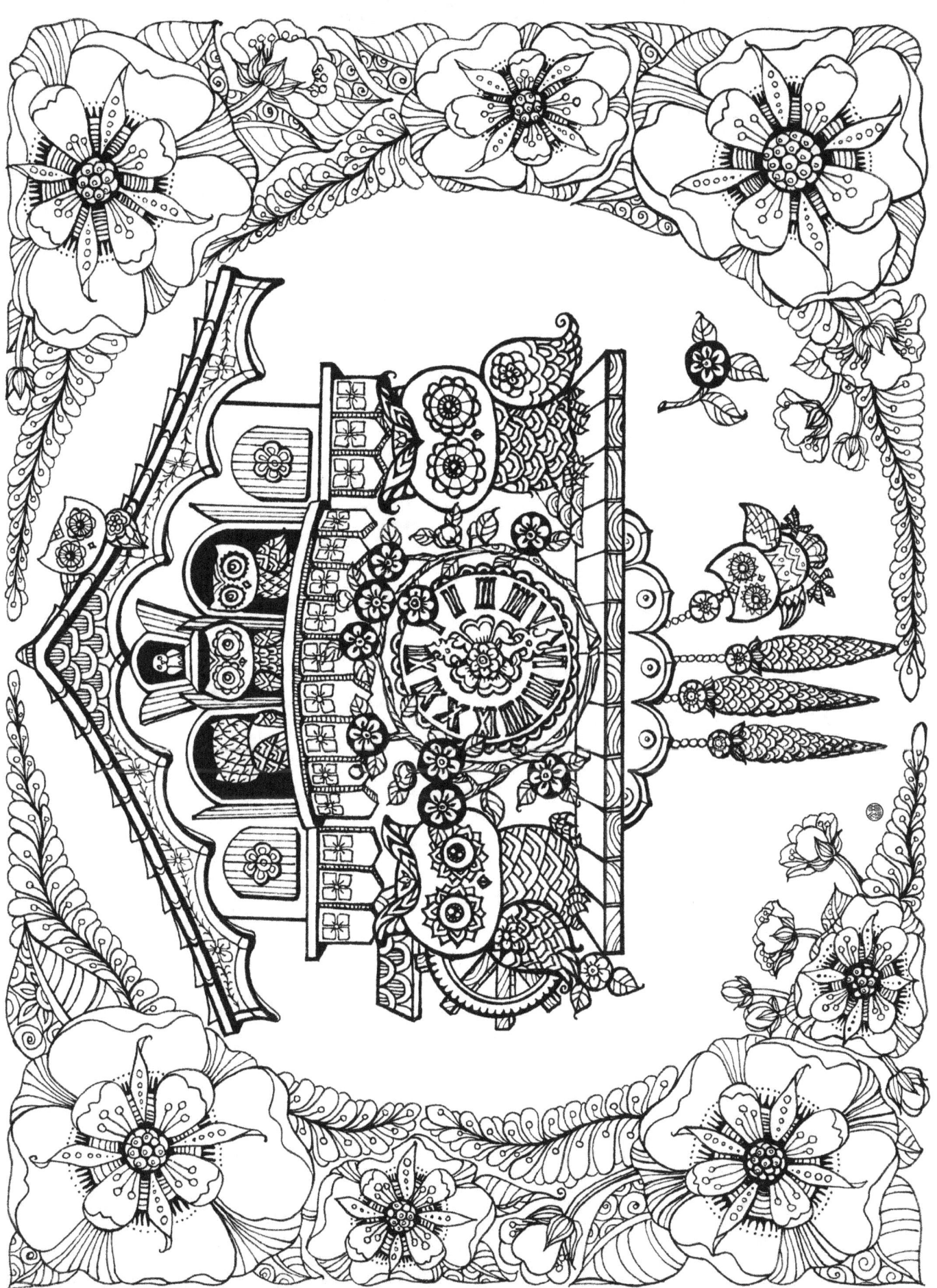

Contributing Artist
Wenyu Lin Small Fish
Taiwan

Facebook : smallfish.smallfish

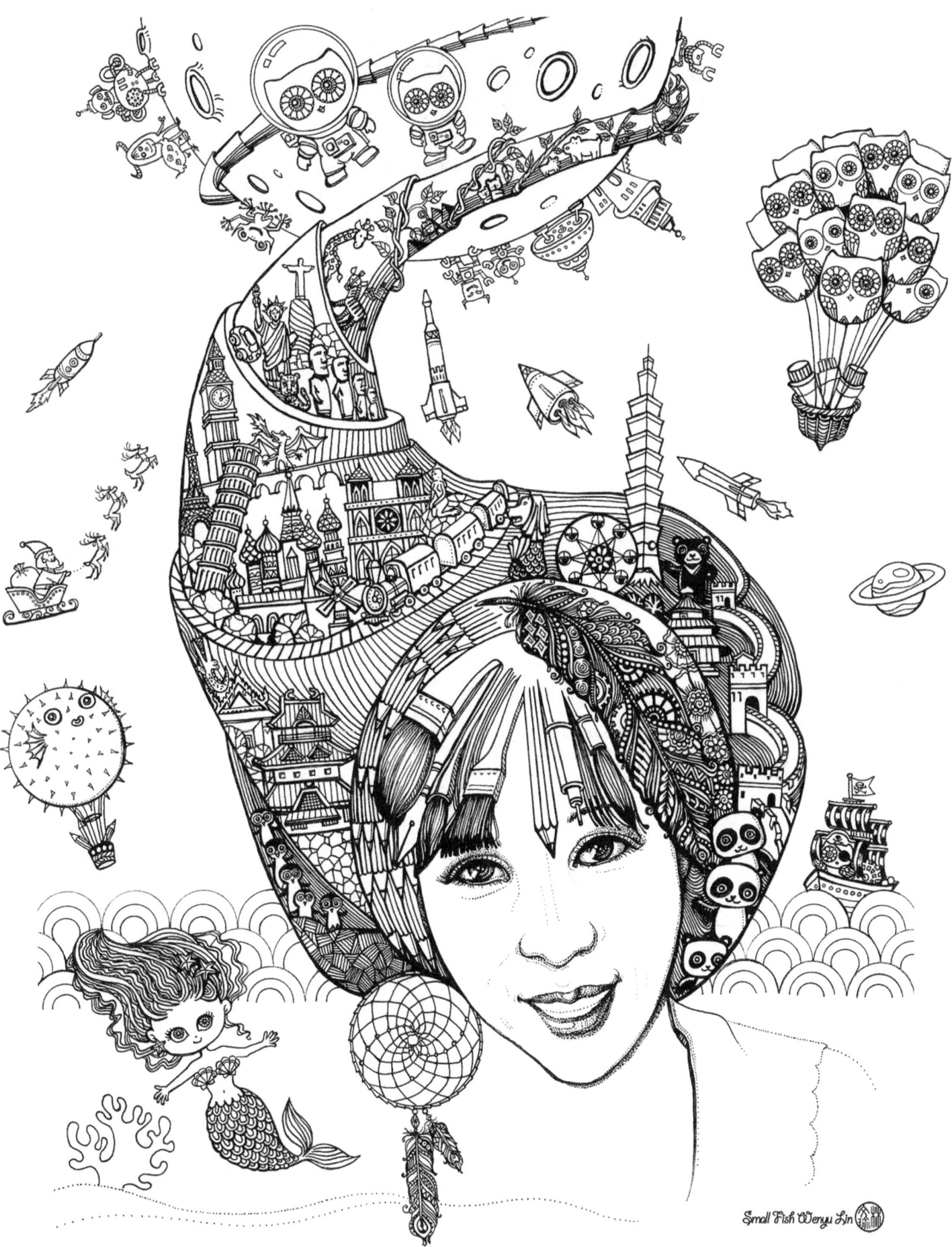

Contributing Artist
Wenyu Lin Small Fish
Taiwan

Facebook : smallfish.smallfish

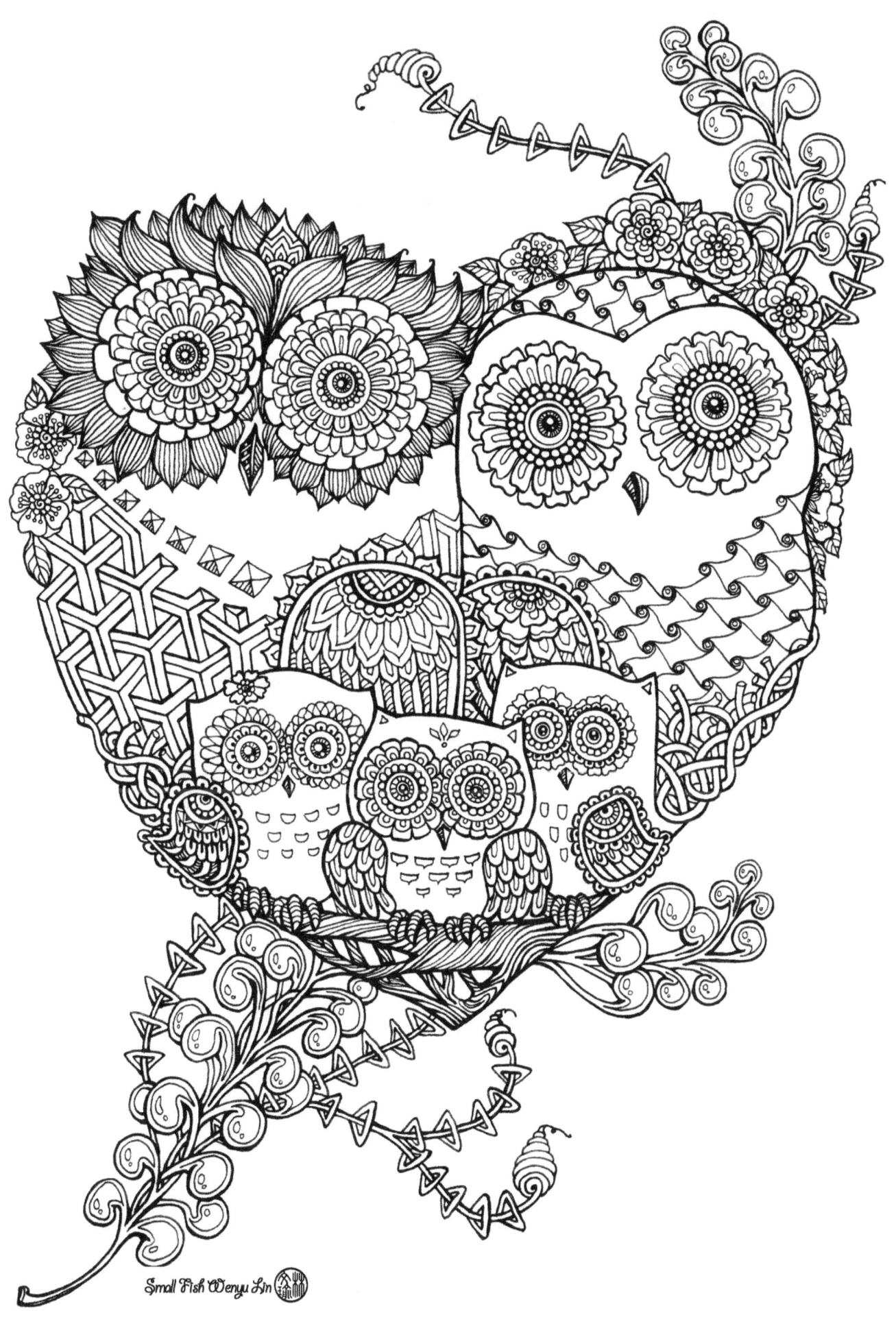

Contributing Artist
Rover Hsiao
Taiwan

Facebook : roverhsiao2015

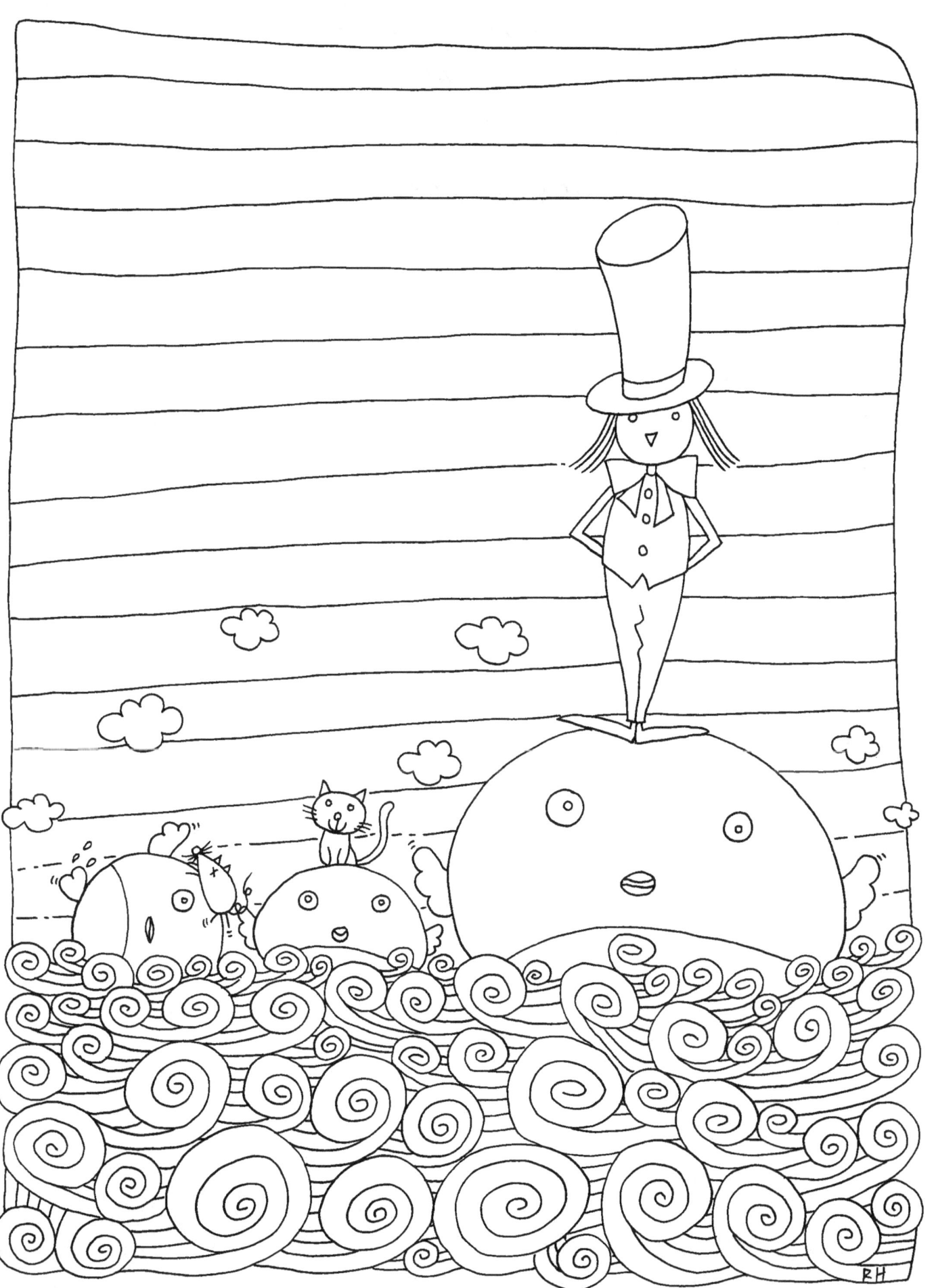

Contributing Artist
Rover Hsiao
Taiwan

Facebook : roverhsiao2015

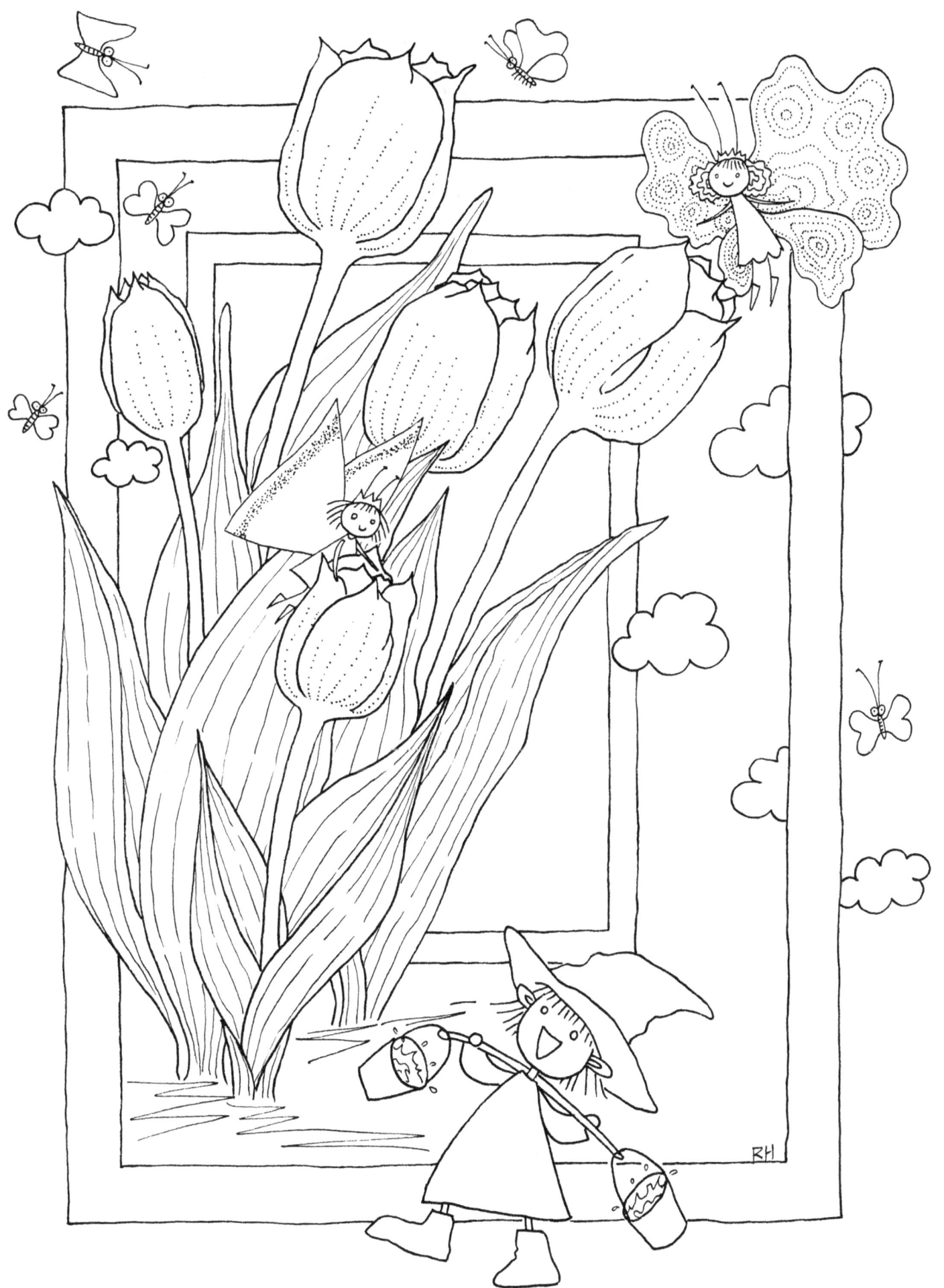

Contributing Artist
Rover Hsiao
Taiwan

Facebook : roverhsiao2015

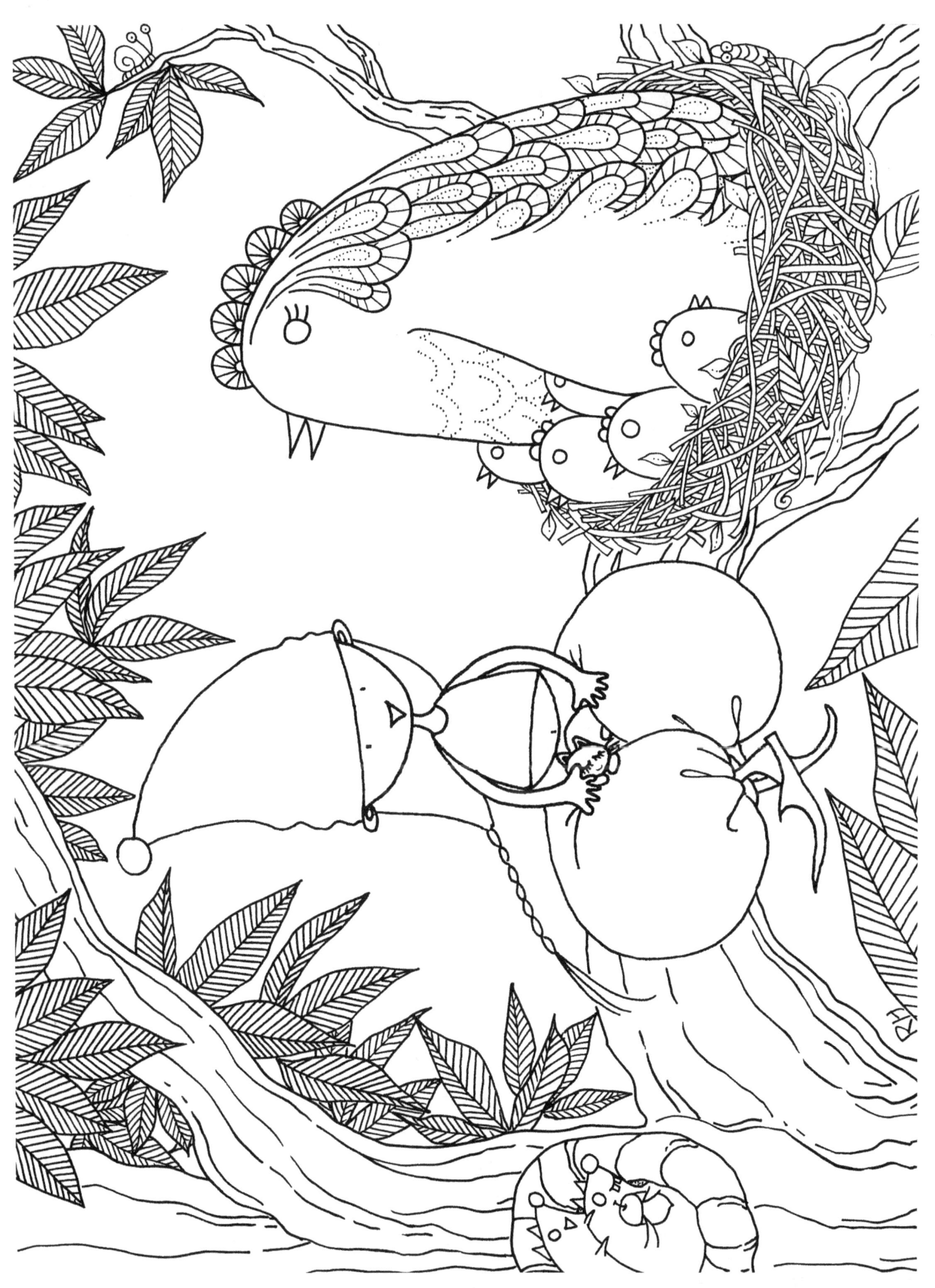

Contributing Artist
Wanting Huang
Taiwan

Facebook : raccoon1220

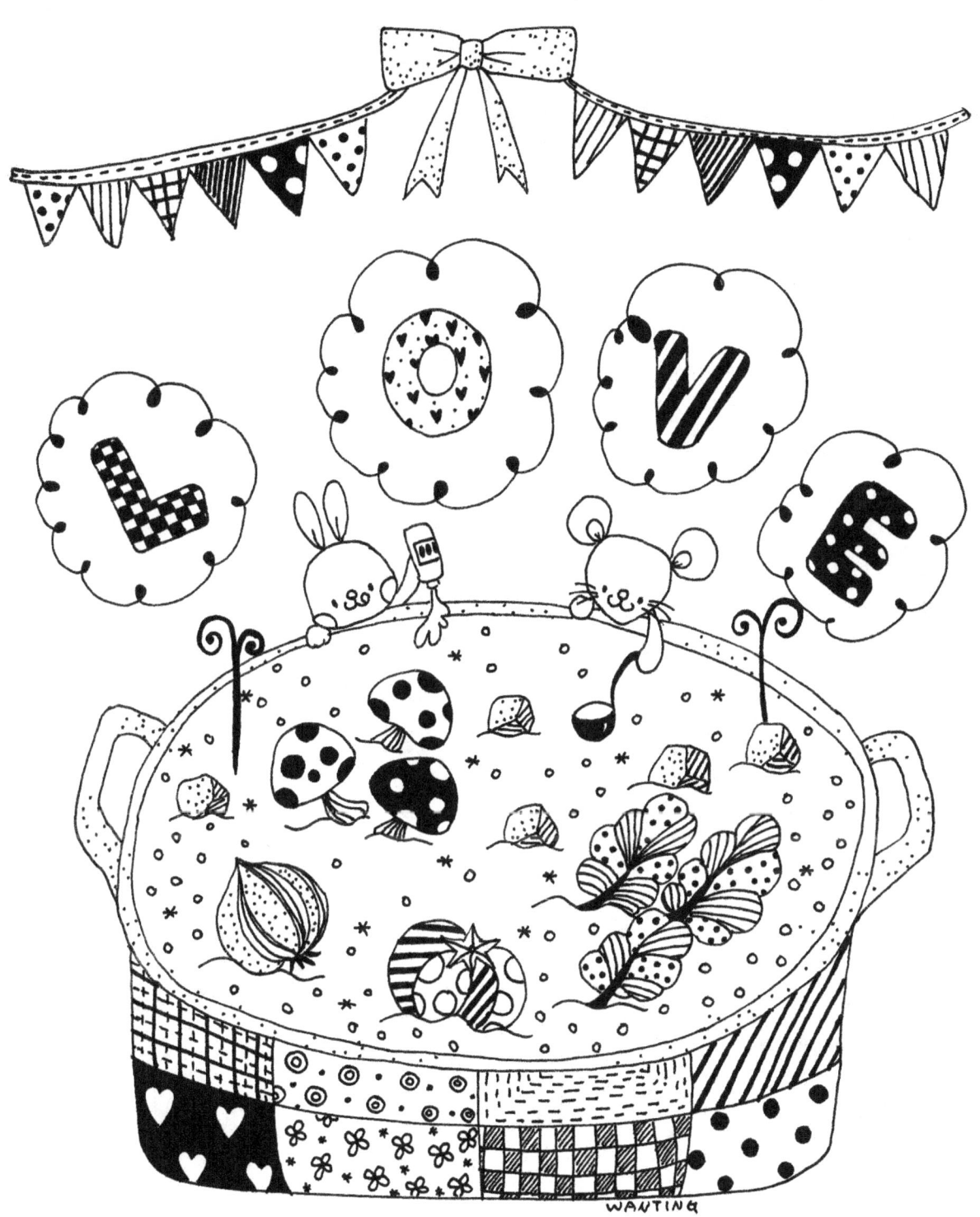

Contributing Artist
Wanting Huang
Taiwan

Facebook : raccoon1220

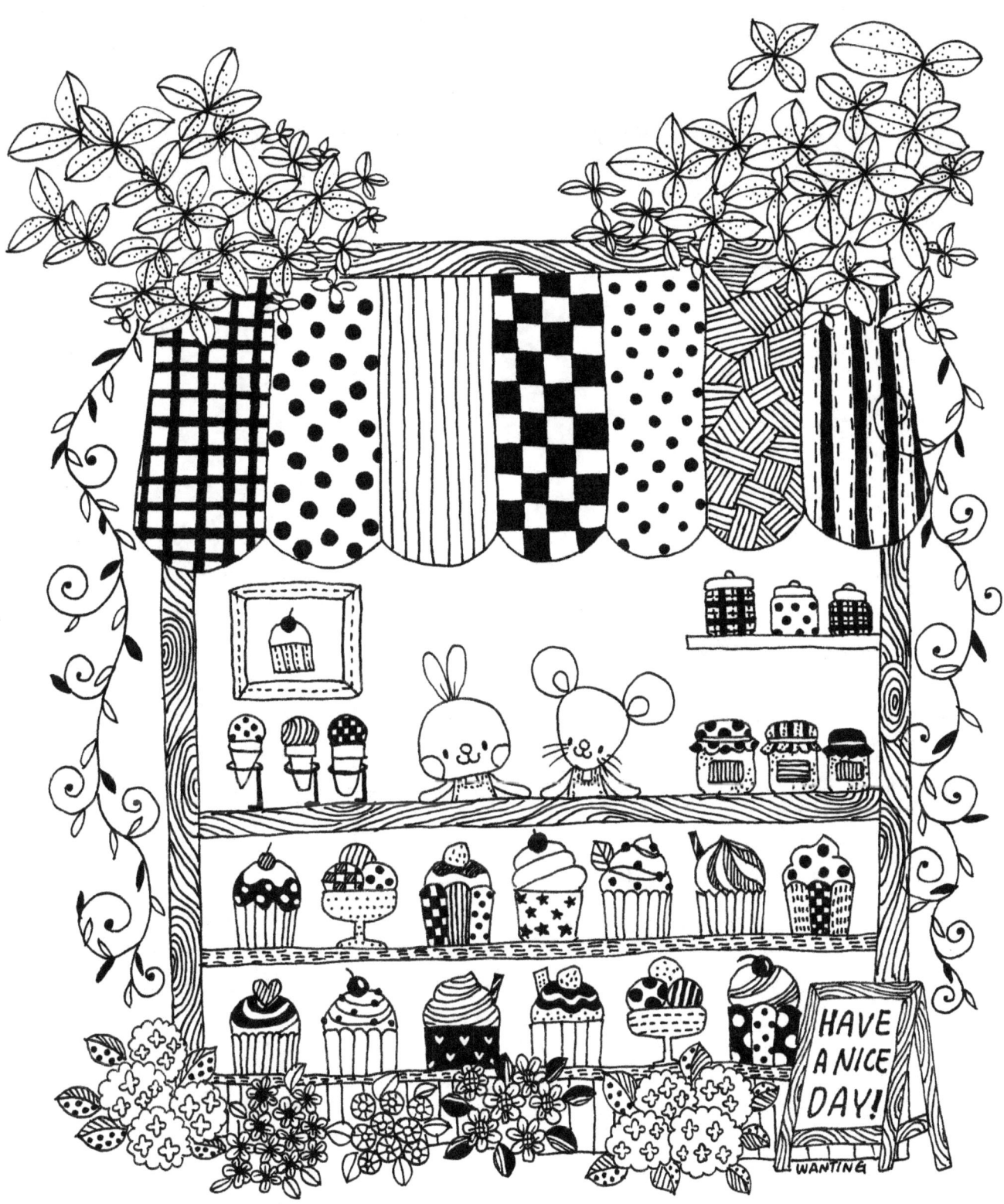

Contributing Artist
Wanting Huang
Taiwan

Facebook : raccoon1220

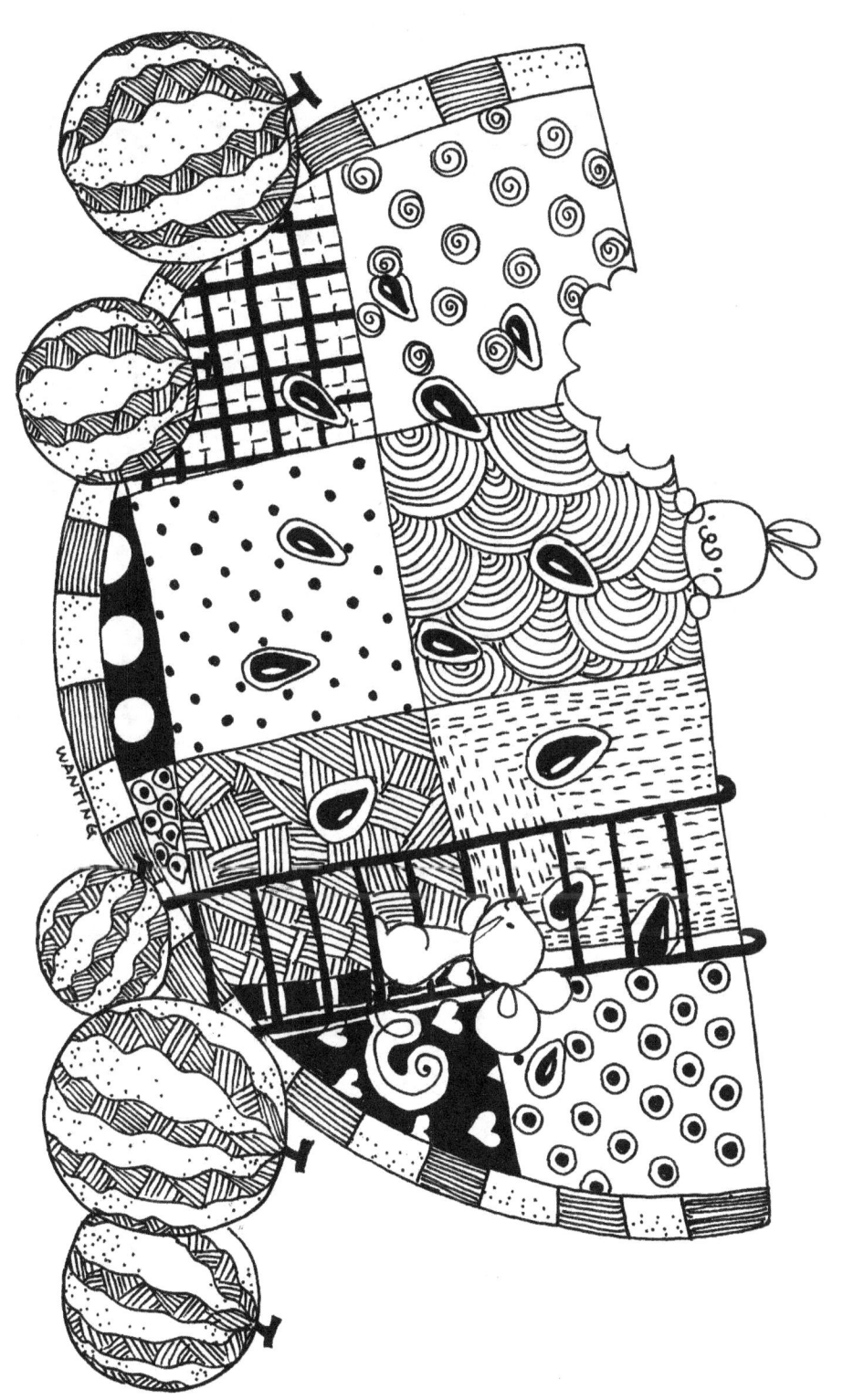

Contributing Artist
Pica Wu
Taiwan

Facebook : picapicadrow2

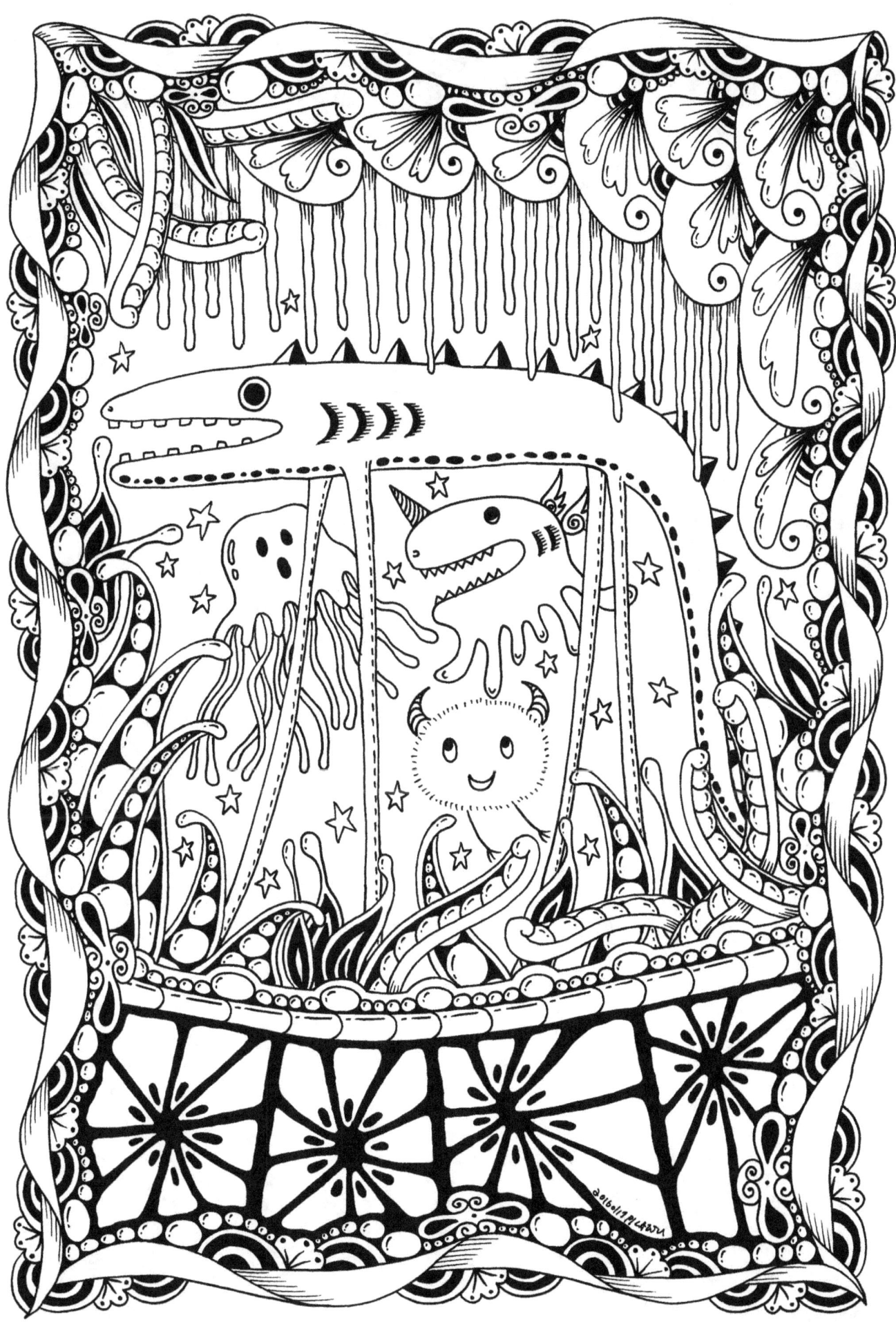

Contributing Artist
Pica Wu
Taiwan

Facebook : picapicadrow2

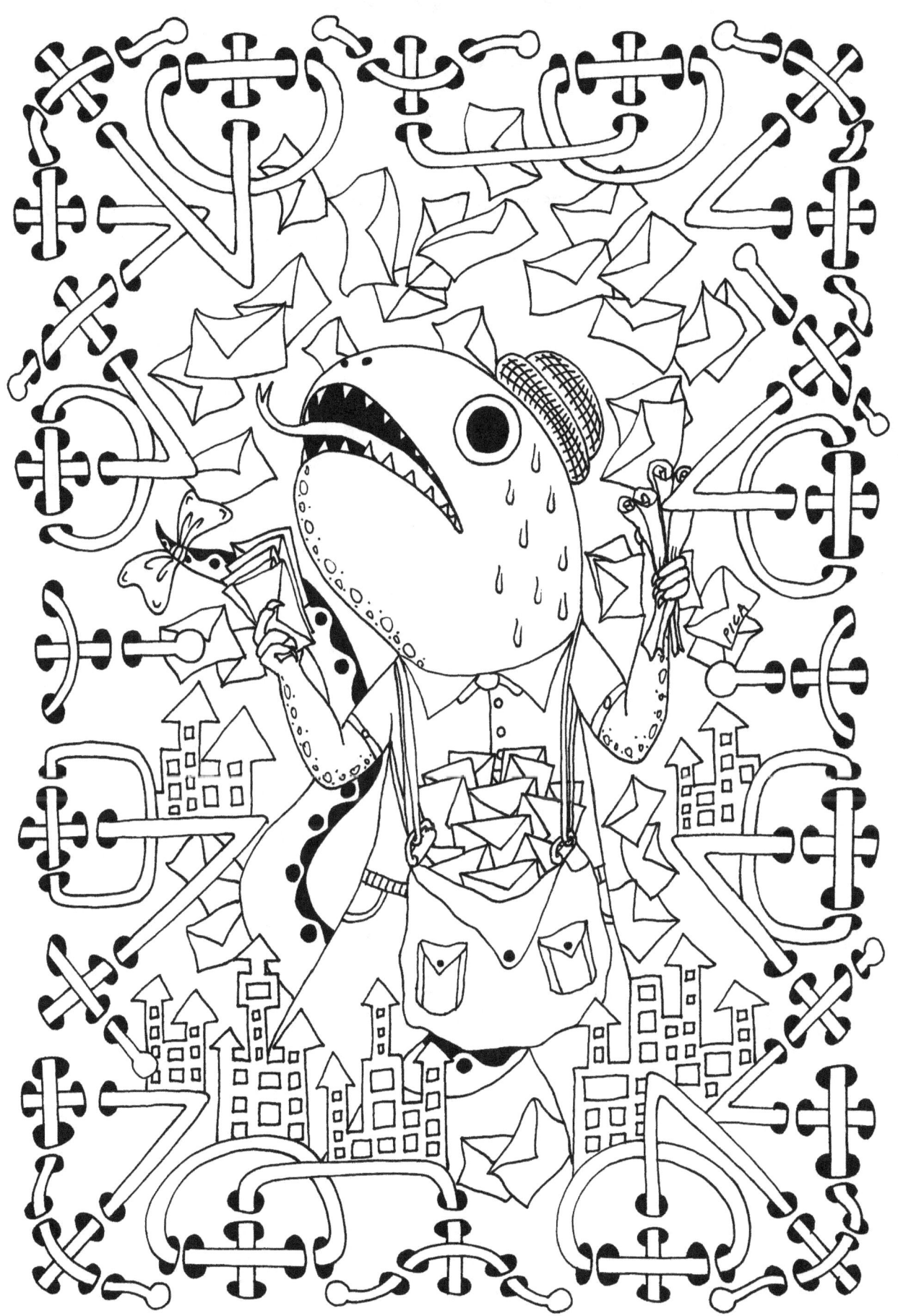

Contributing Artist
Pica Wu
Taiwan

Facebook : picapicadrow2

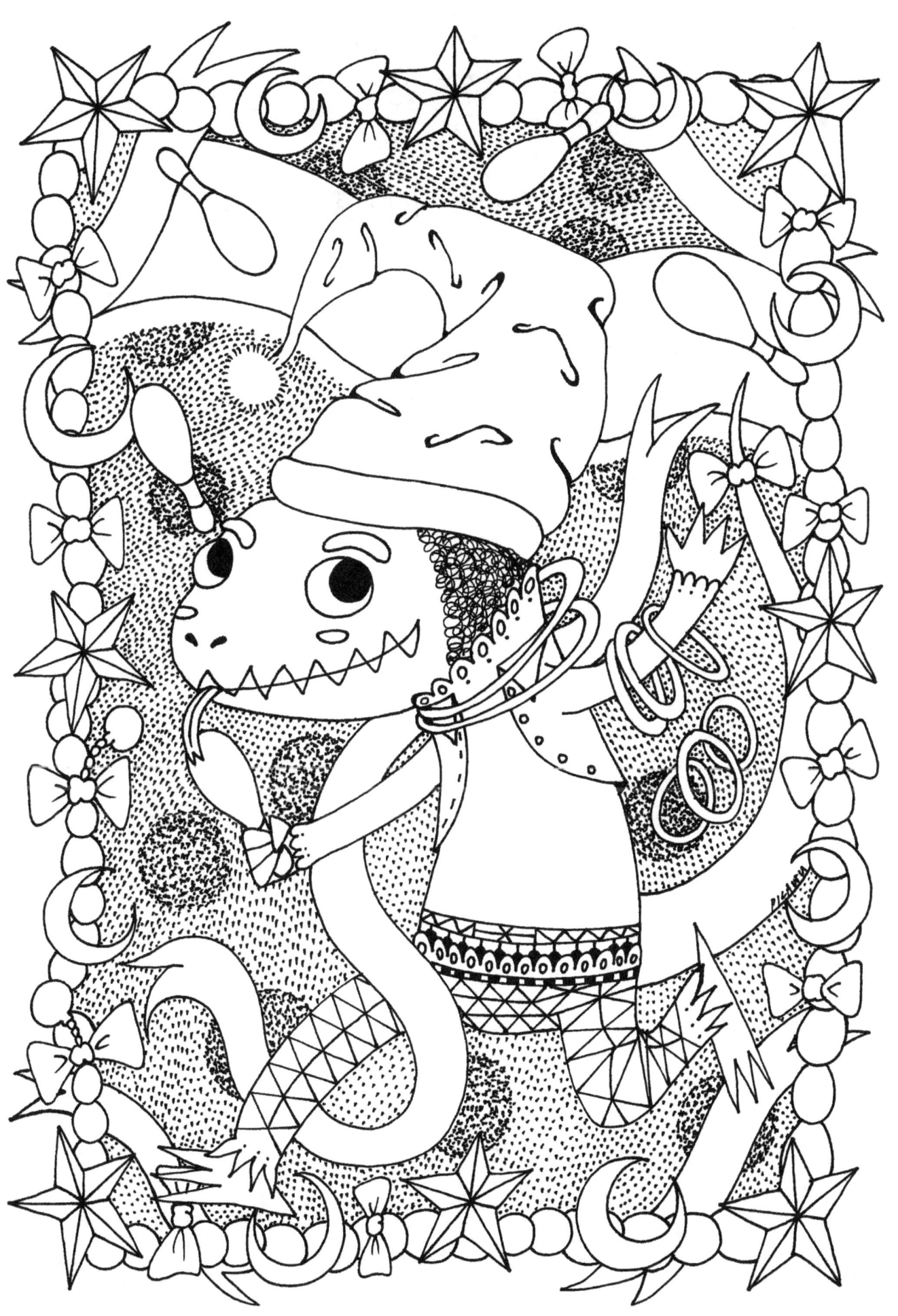

Contributing Artist
Nancy43
Taiwan

Facebook : 43Nancy43

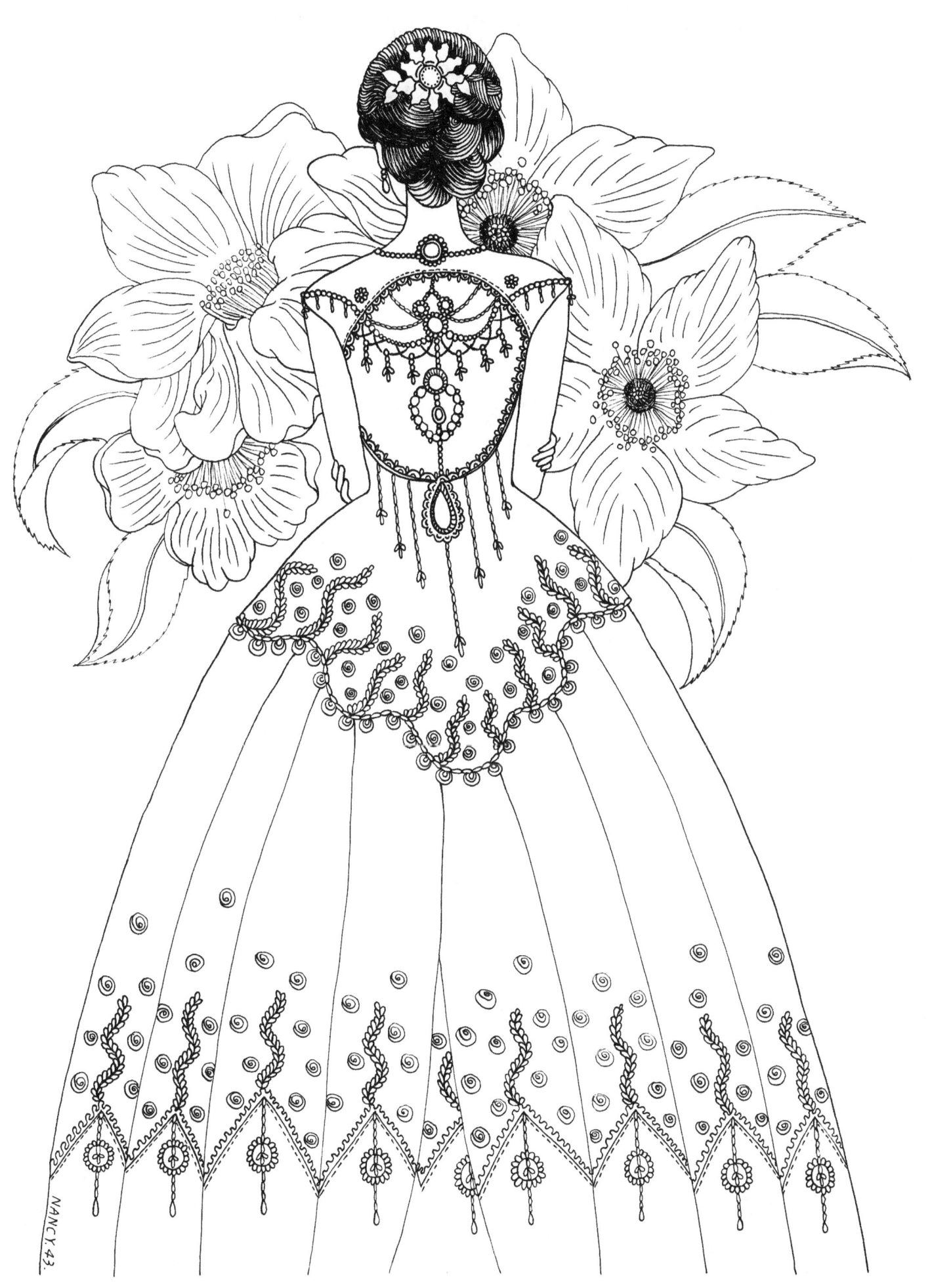

Contributing Artist
Nancy43
Taiwan

Facebook : 43Nancy43

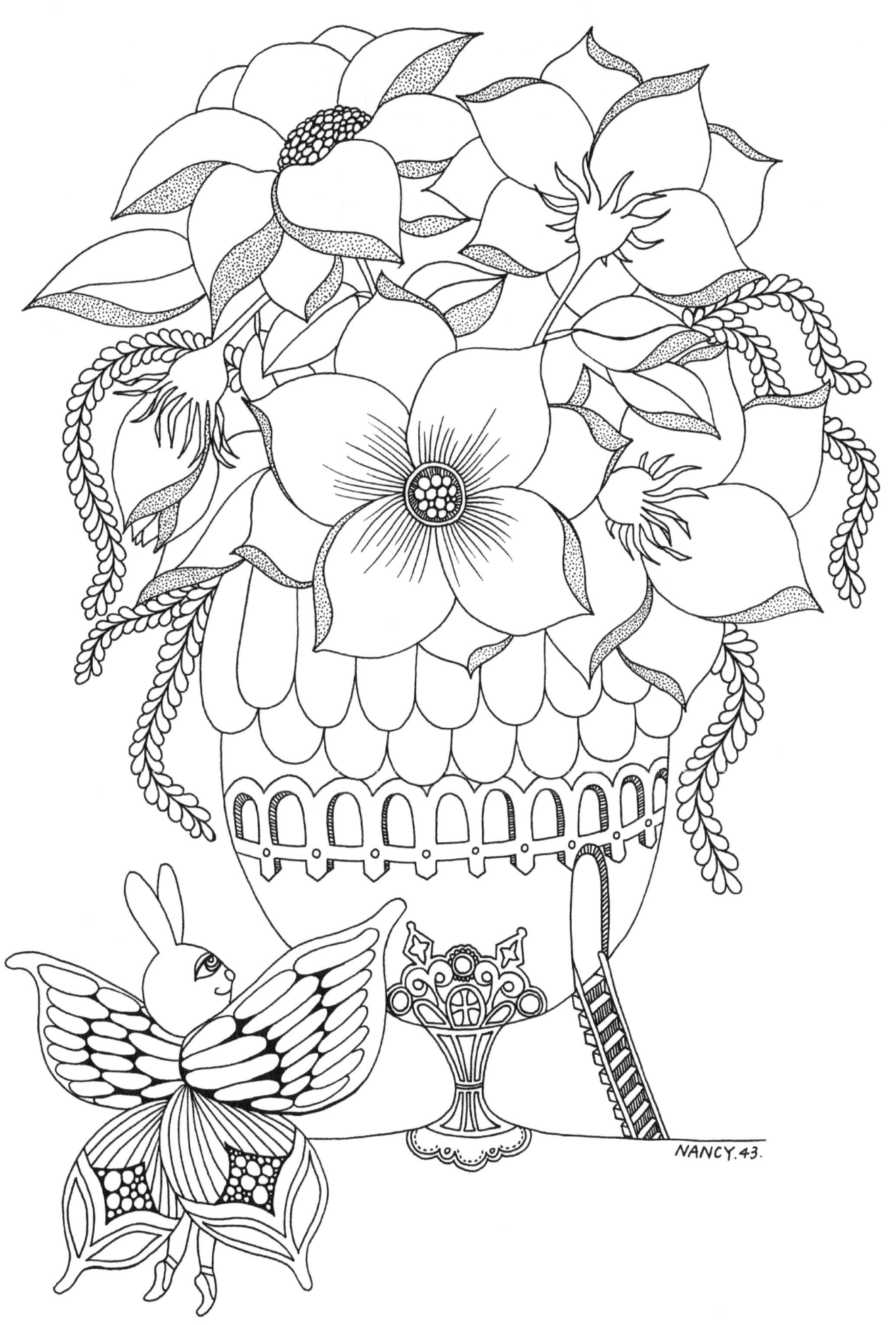

Contributing Artist
Nancy43
Taiwan

Facebook : 43Nancy43

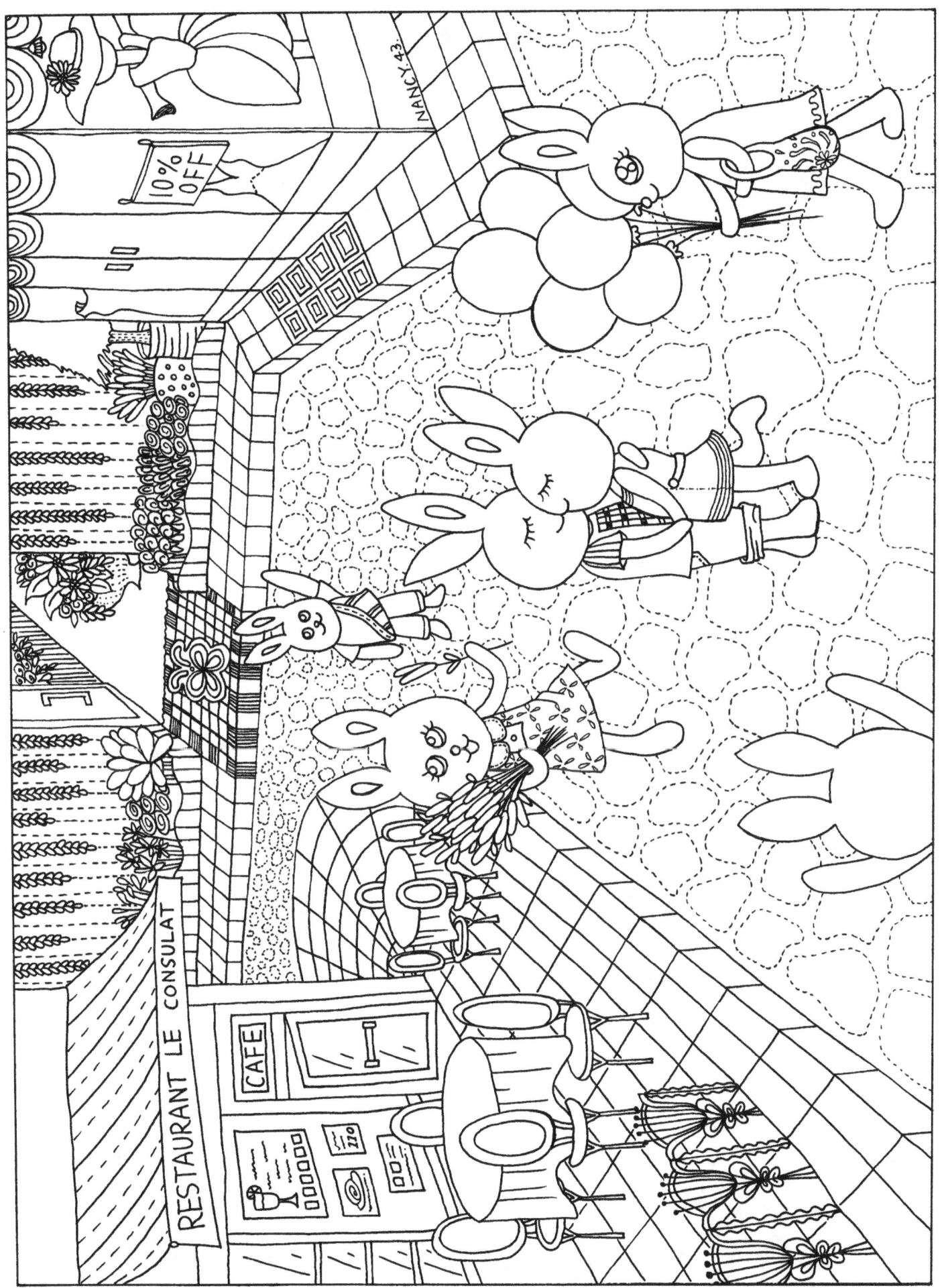

Contributing Artist
Lilan Chen
Taiwan

Facebook : lilanchen.art

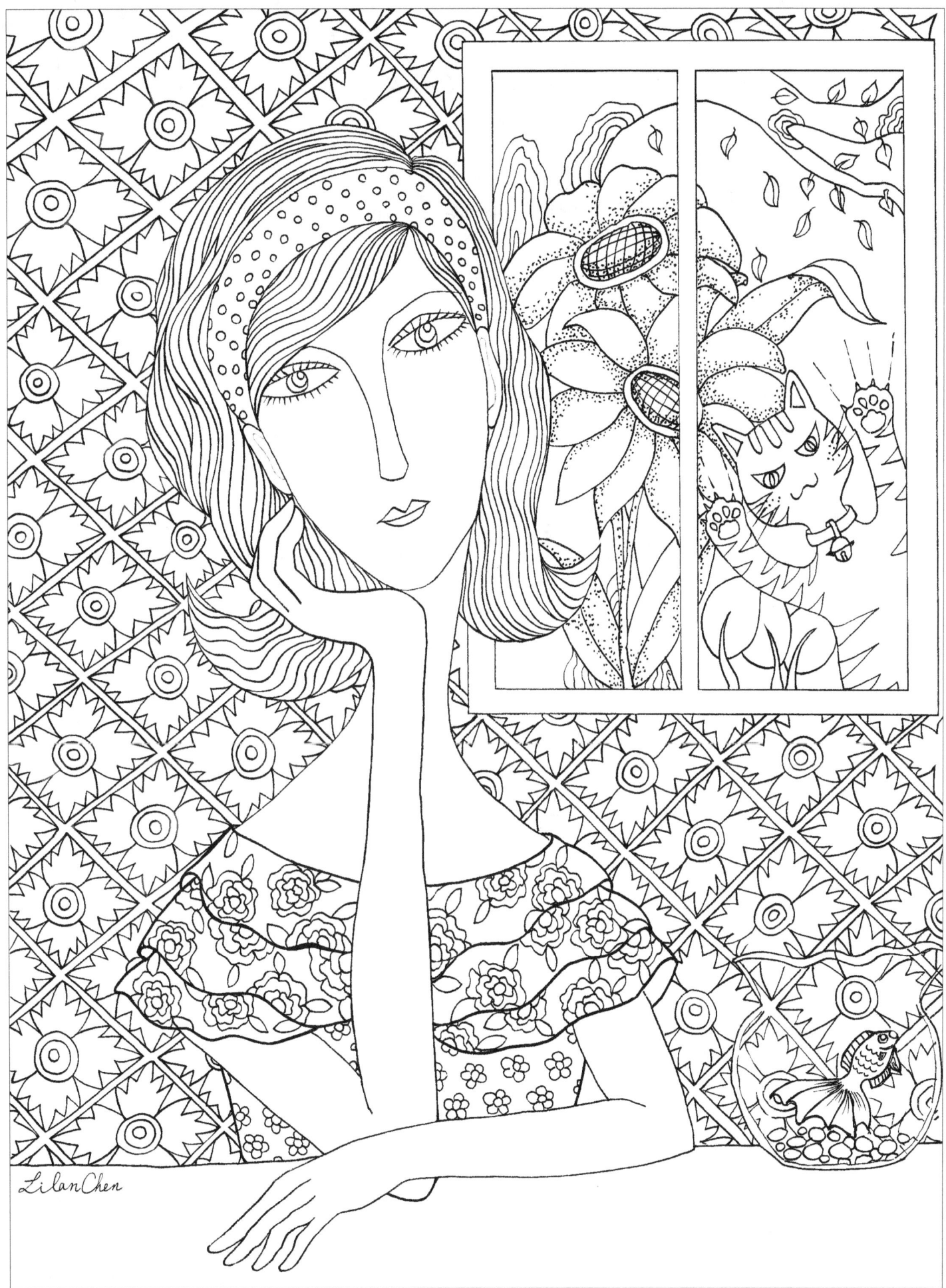

Contributing Artist
Lilan Chen
Taiwan

Facebook : lilanchen.art

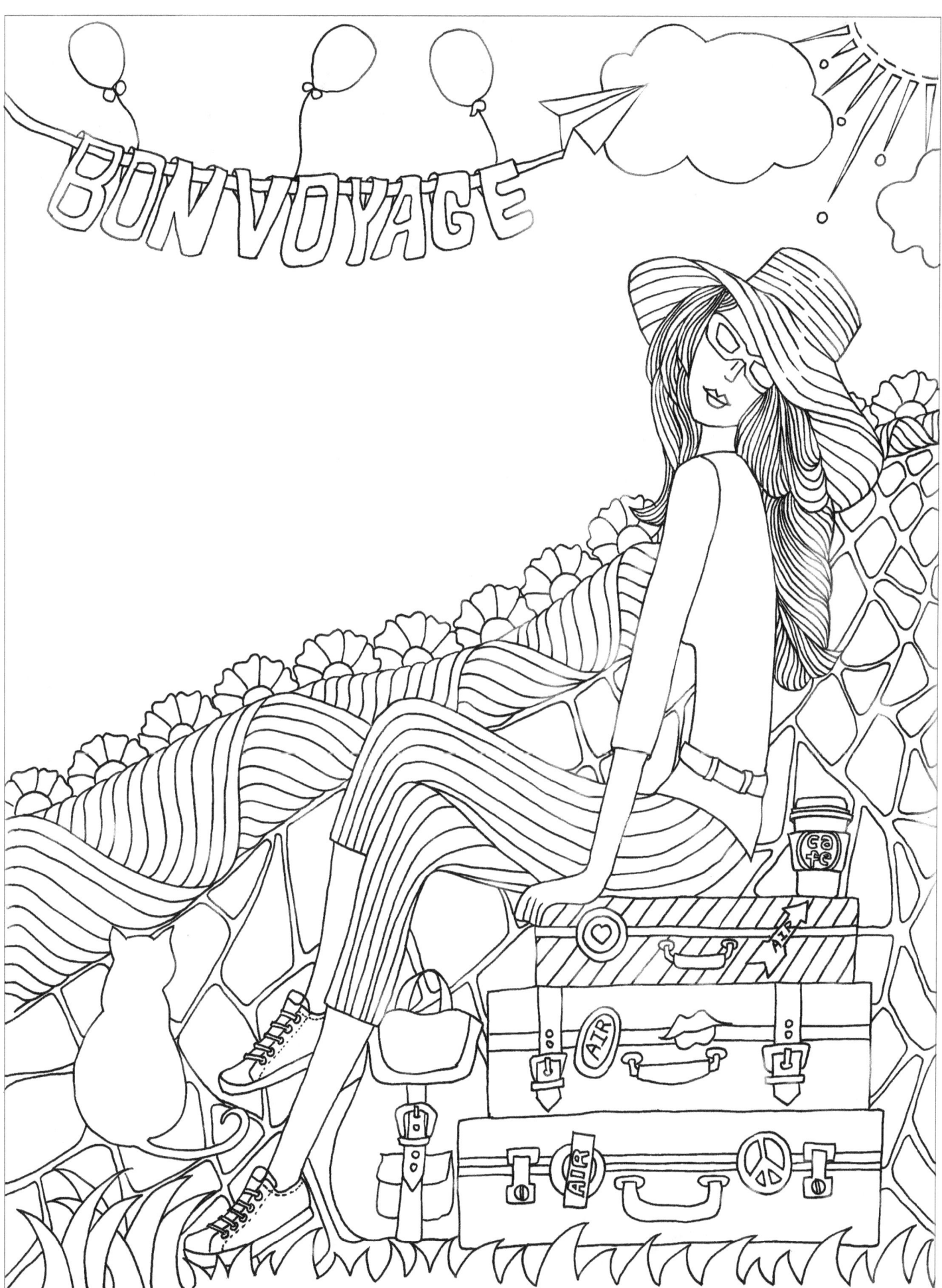

Contributing Artist
Lilan Chen
Taiwan

Facebook : lilanchen.art

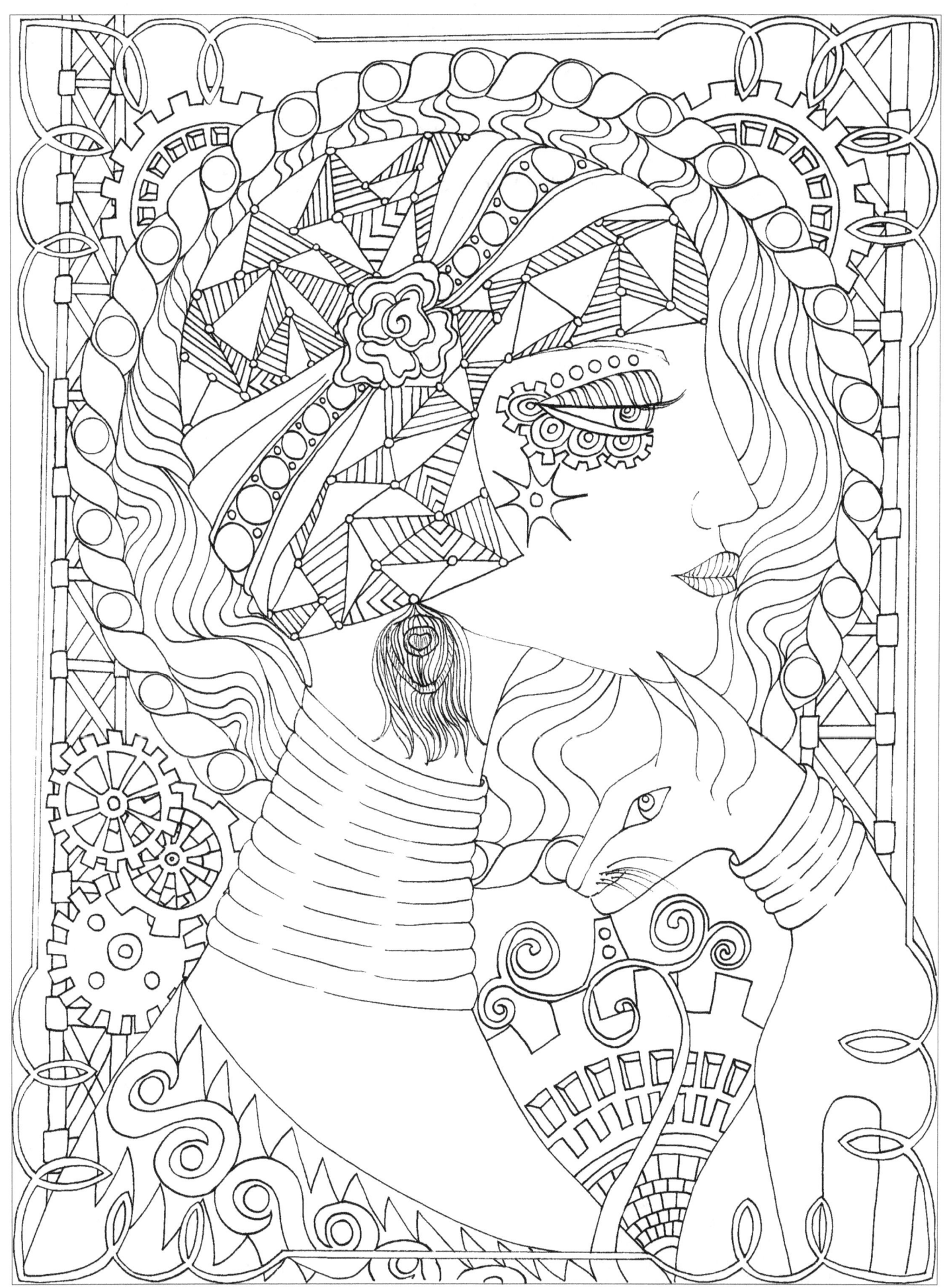

Contributing Artist
Maggie Lin
Taiwan

Facebook : maggiezentangle

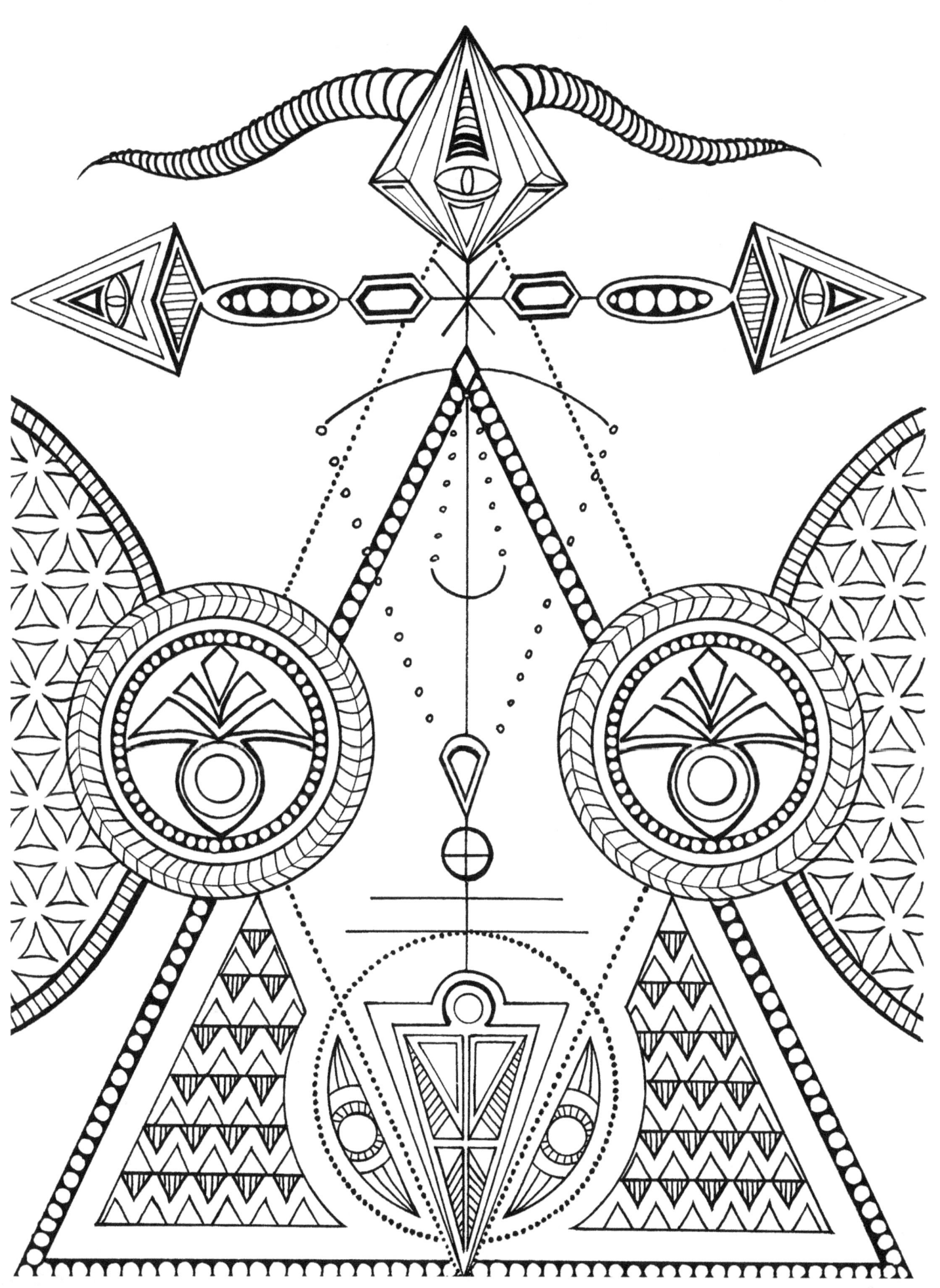

Contributing Artist
Maggie Lin
Taiwan

Facebook : maggiezentangle

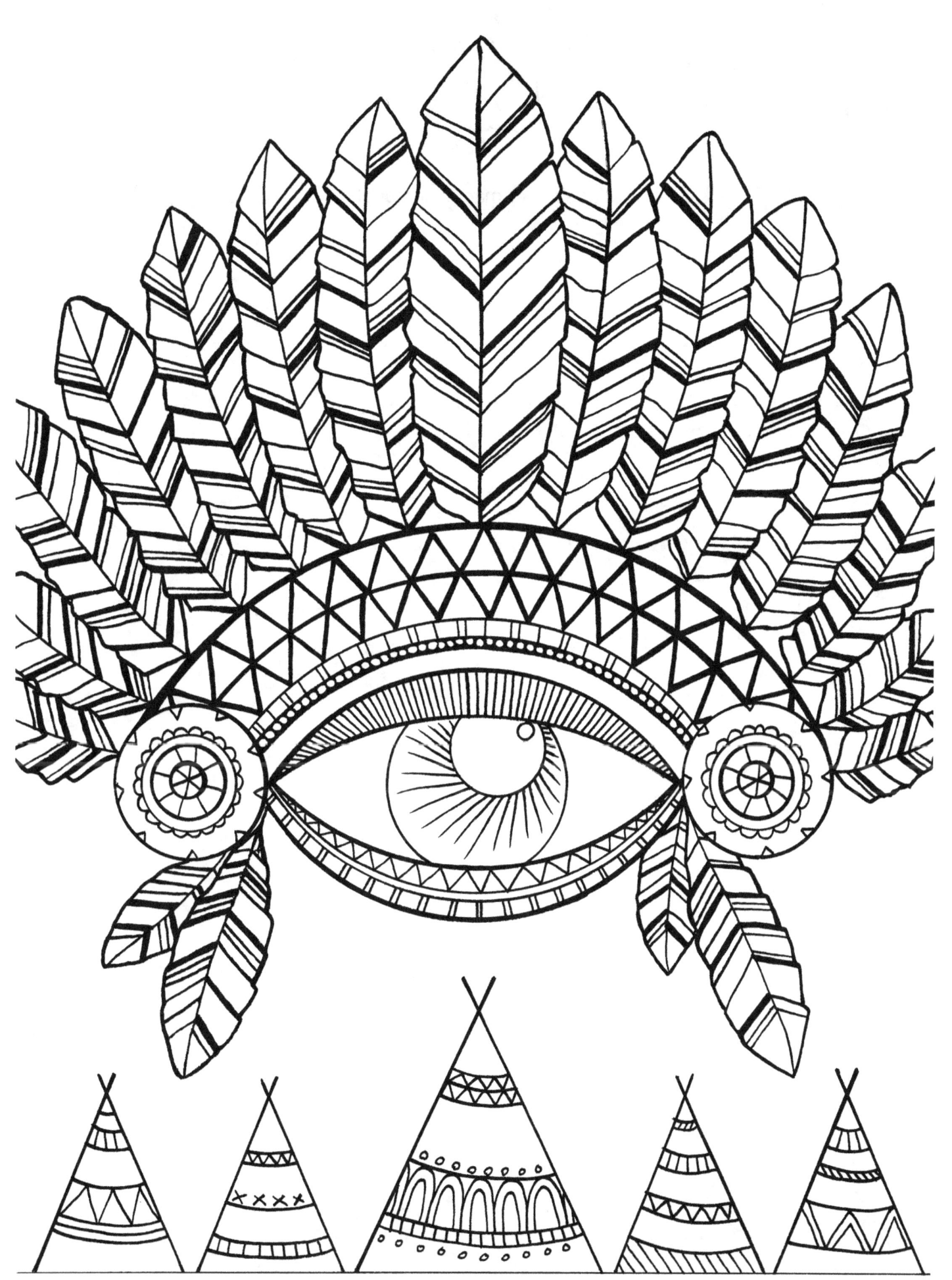

Contributing Artist
Maggie Lin
Taiwan

Facebook : maggiezentangle

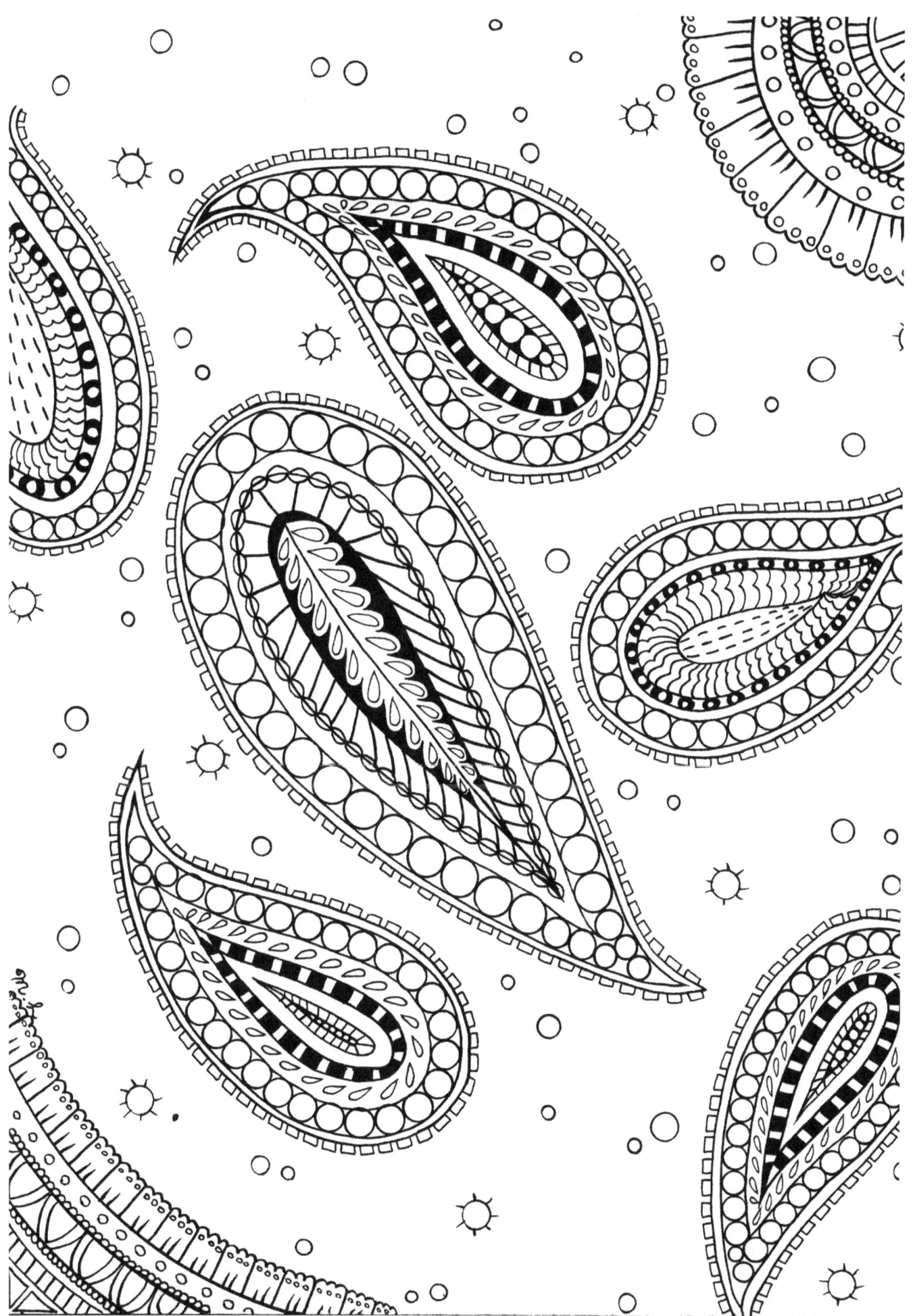

Contributing Artist
Chou Yu-Jin
Taiwan

Facebook : YuJinHandCraftCreation

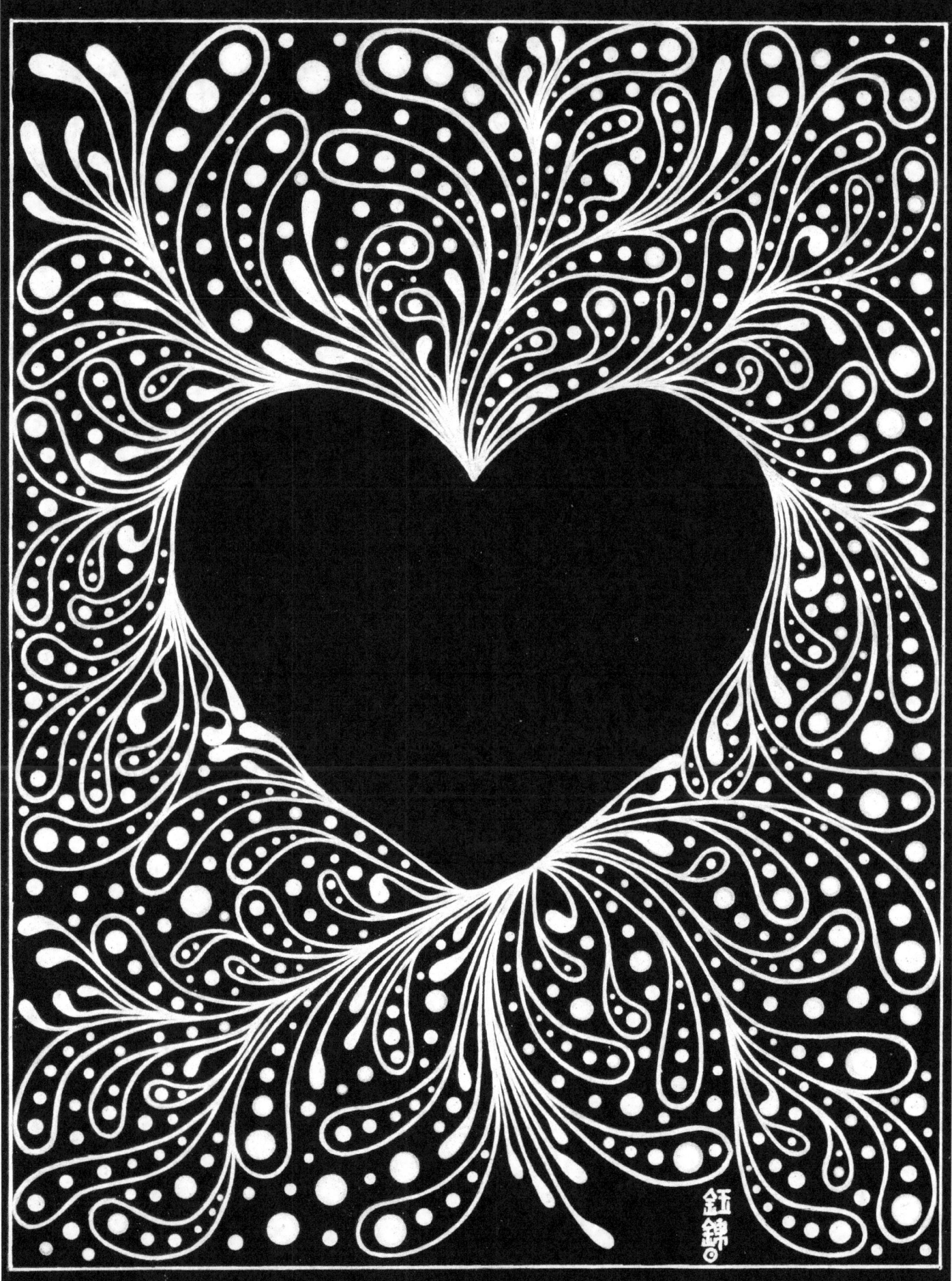

Contributing Artist
Chou Yu-Jin
Taiwan

Facebook : YuJinHandCraftCreation

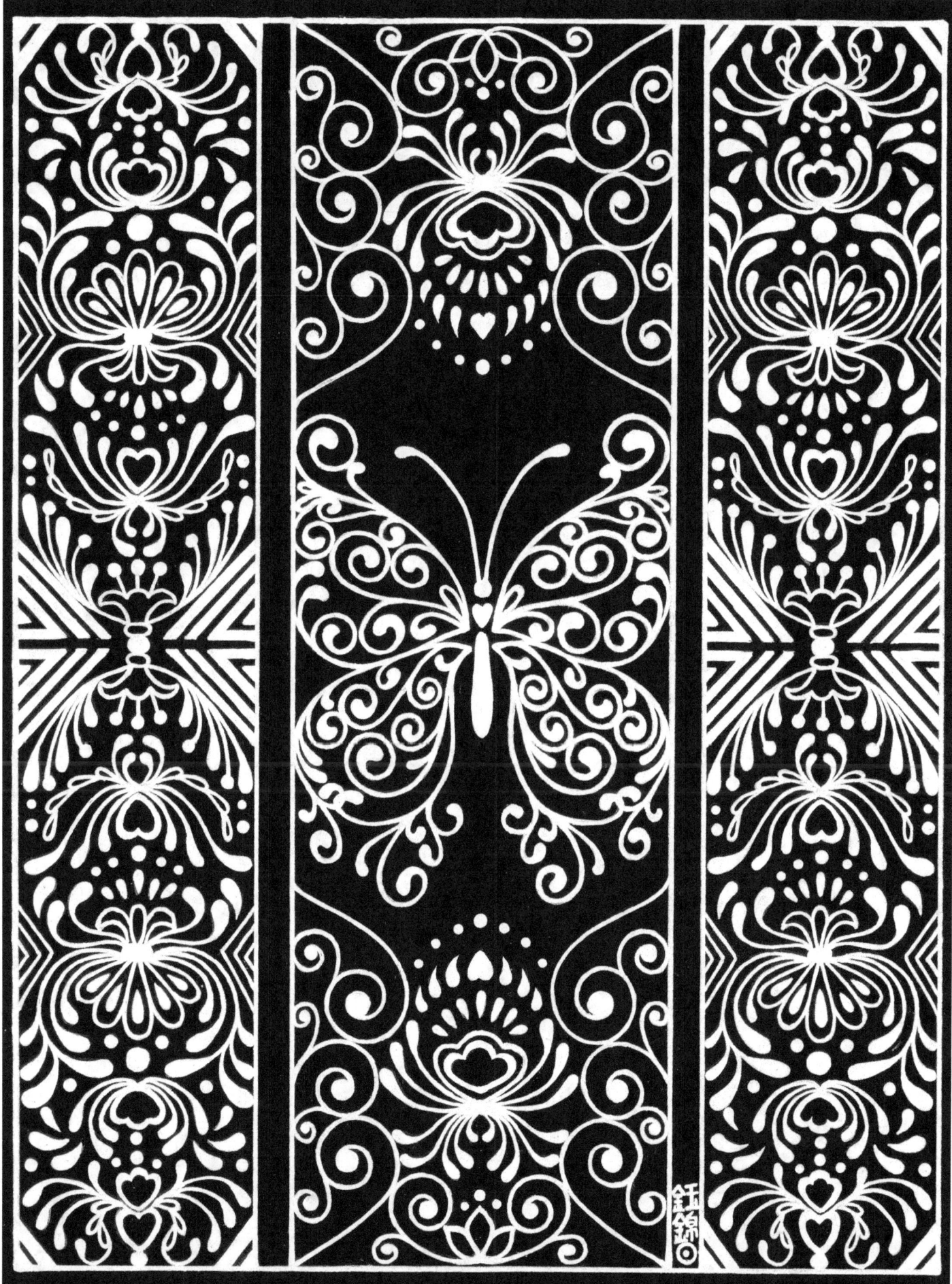

Contributing Artist
Angel Huang
Taiwan

Facebook : An99.Art

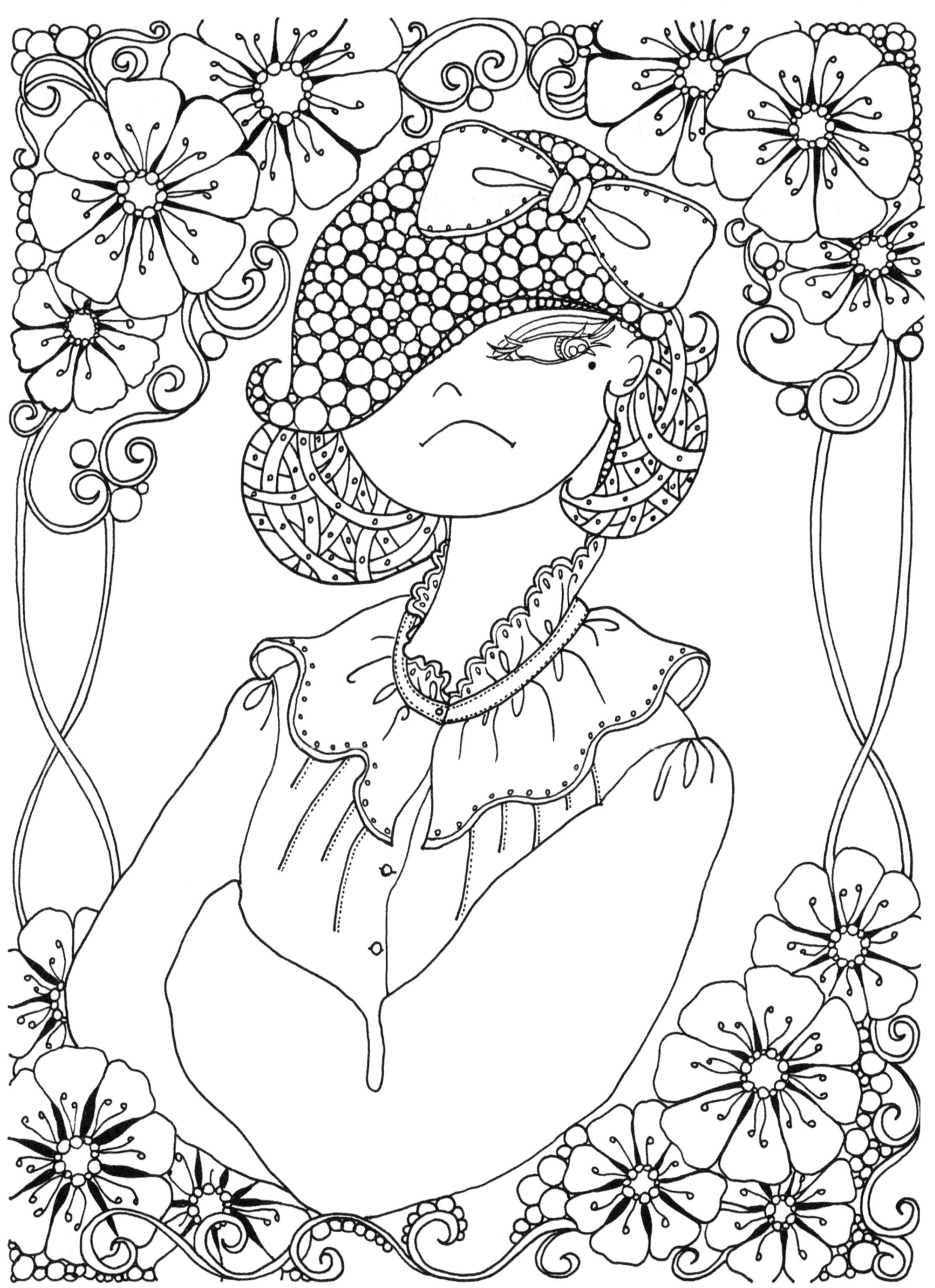

Contributing Artist
Angel Huang
Taiwan

Facebook : An99.Art

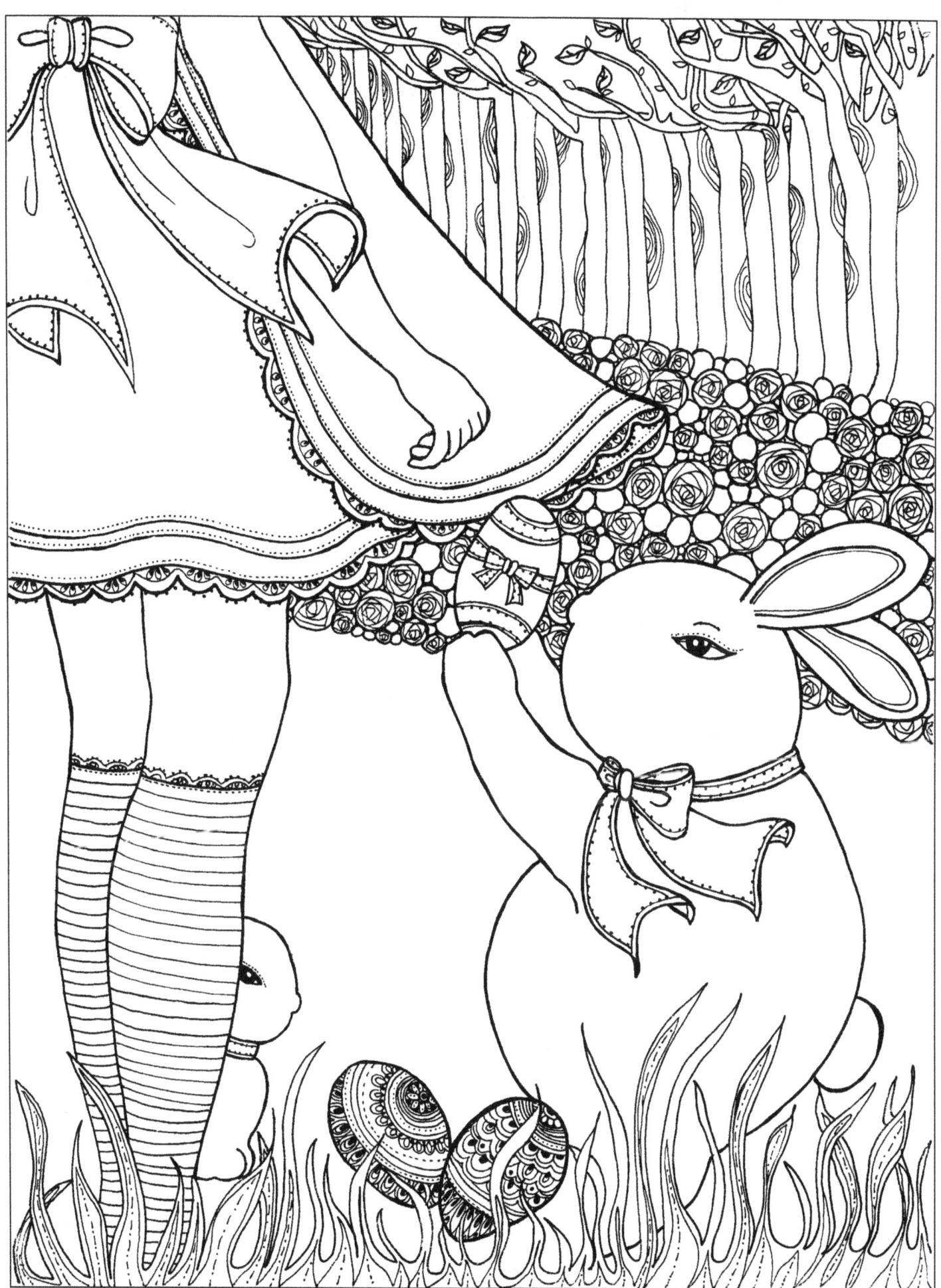

Contributing Artist
Happy Fishhhhh
Taiwan

Facebook : Happy.Fishhhhh

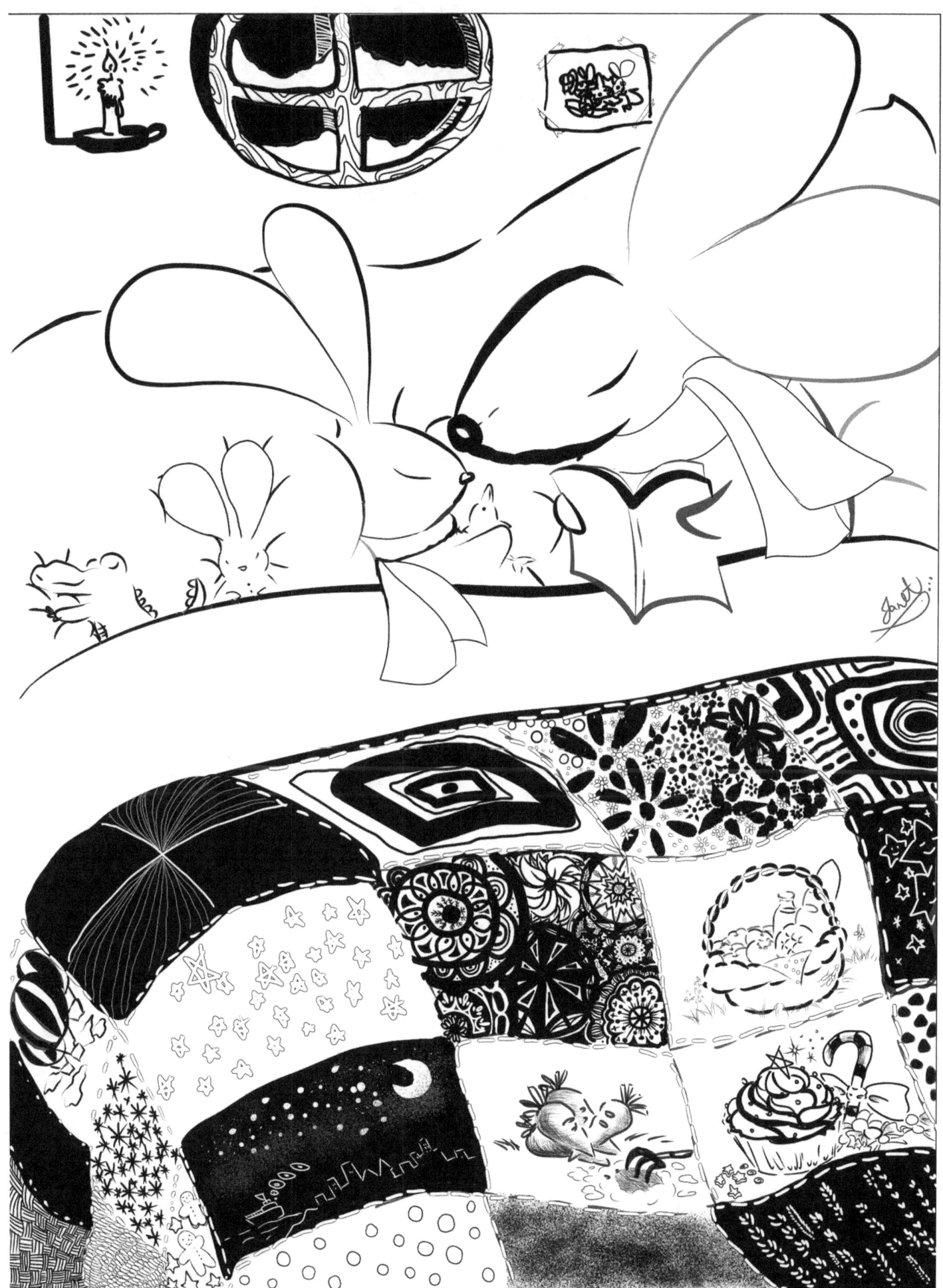

Contributing Artist
Happy Fishhhhh
Taiwan

Facebook : Happy.Fishhhhh

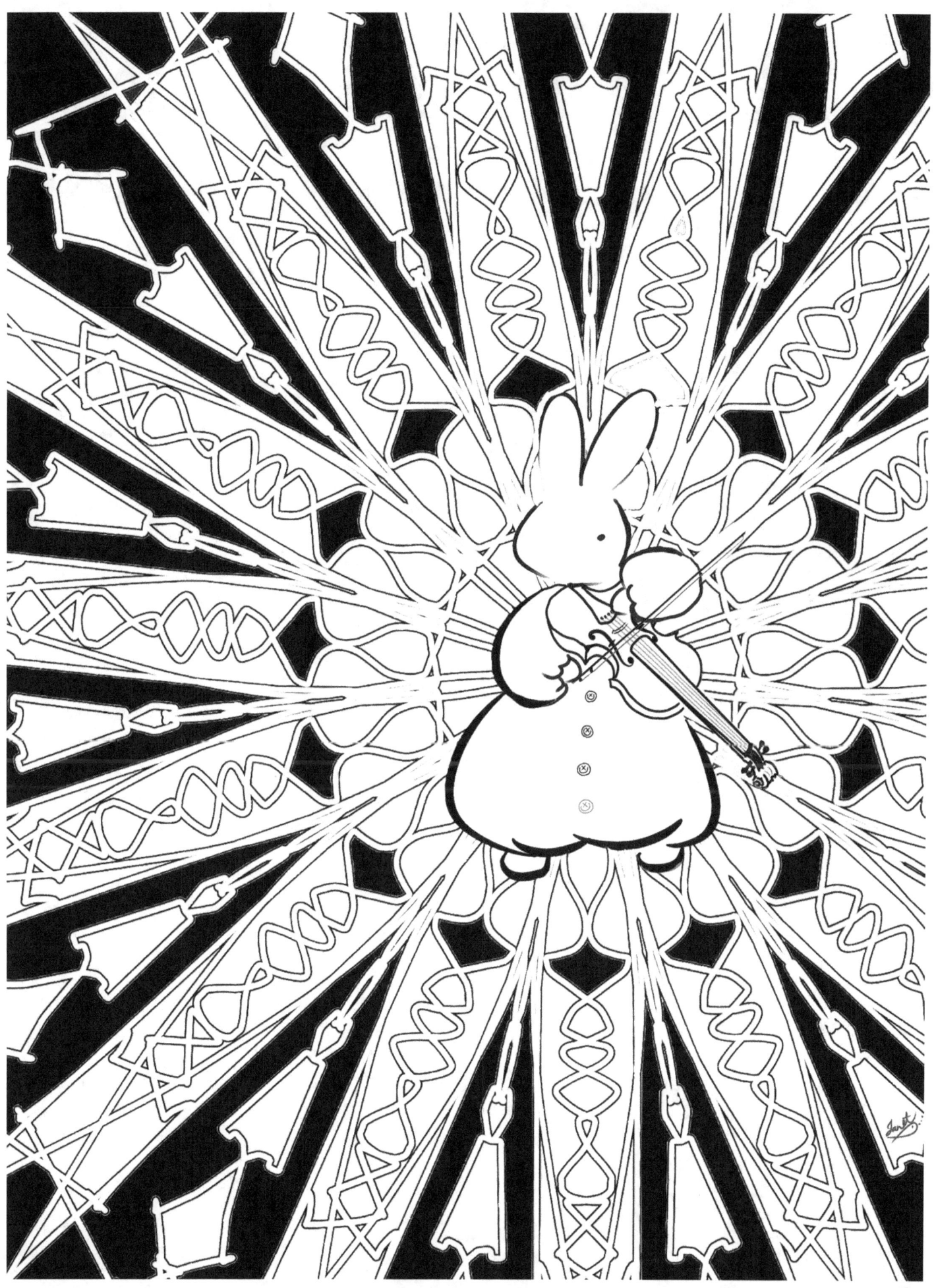

Contributing Artist
Leaf Yeh
Taiwan

Facebook : leaf.Painting

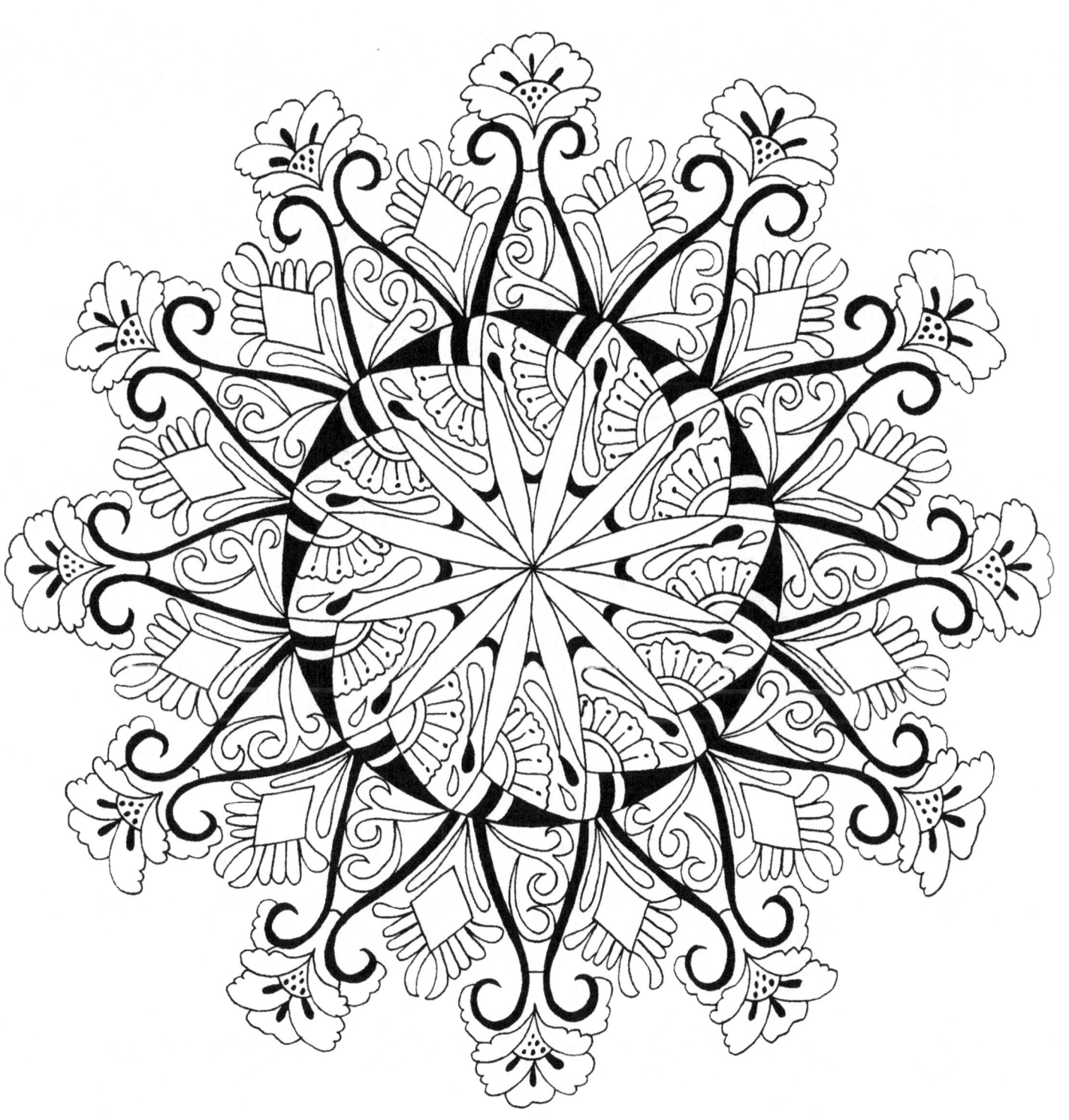

Contributing Artist
Leaf Yeh
Taiwan

Facebook : leaf.Painting

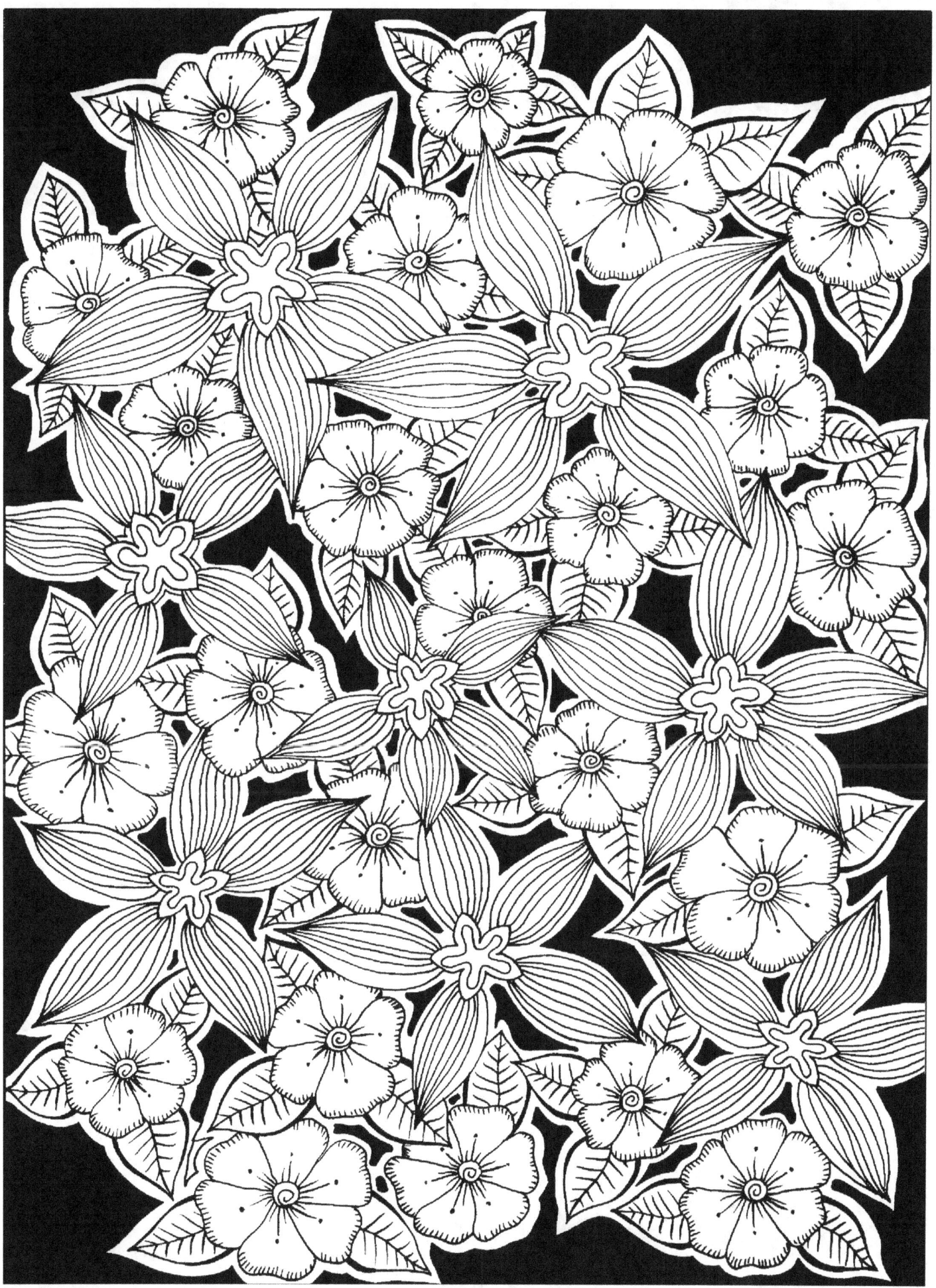

Contributing Artist
Jodi Ho
Taiwan

Facebook : riverho1688

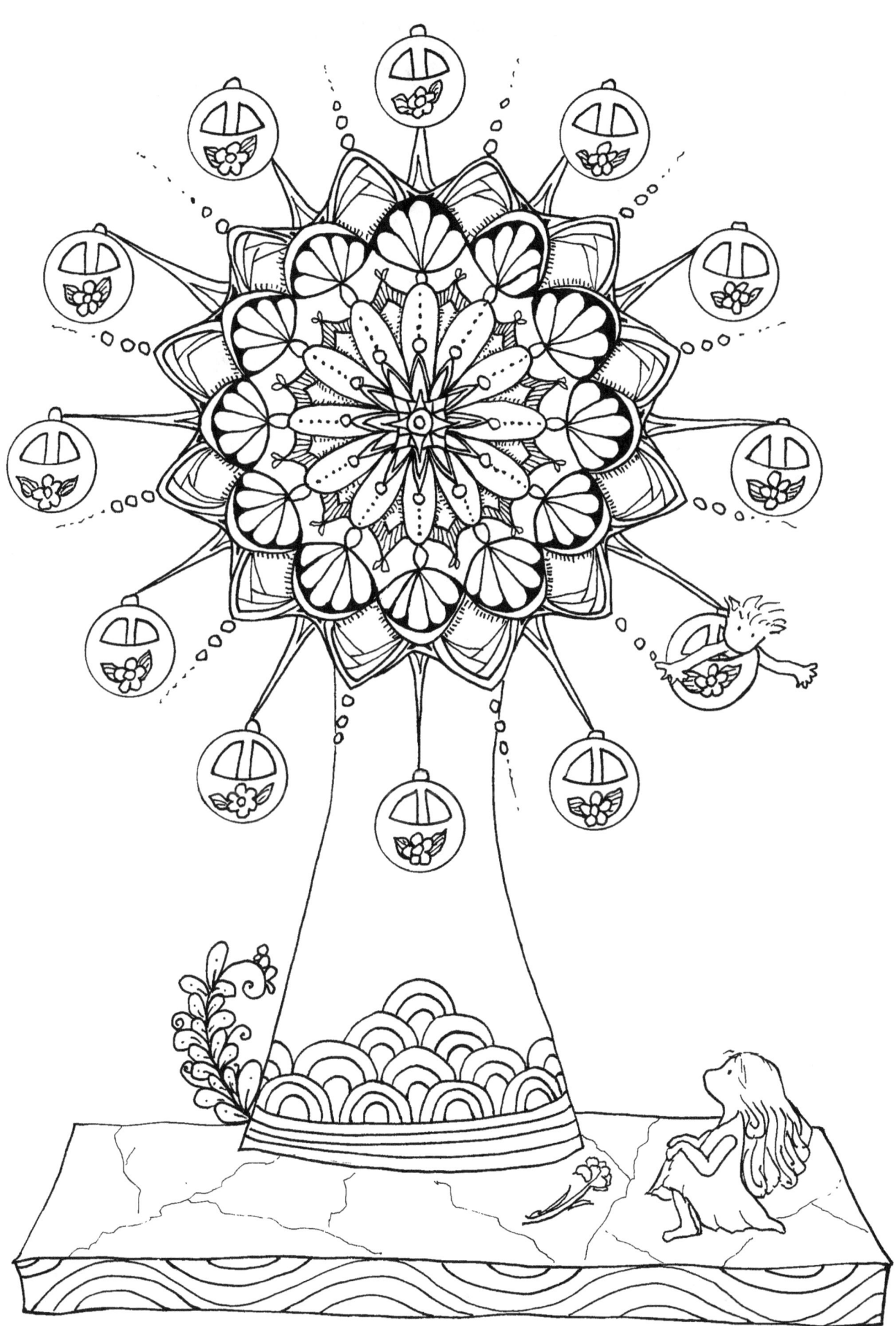

Contributing Artist
Jodi Ho
Taiwan

Facebook : riverho1688

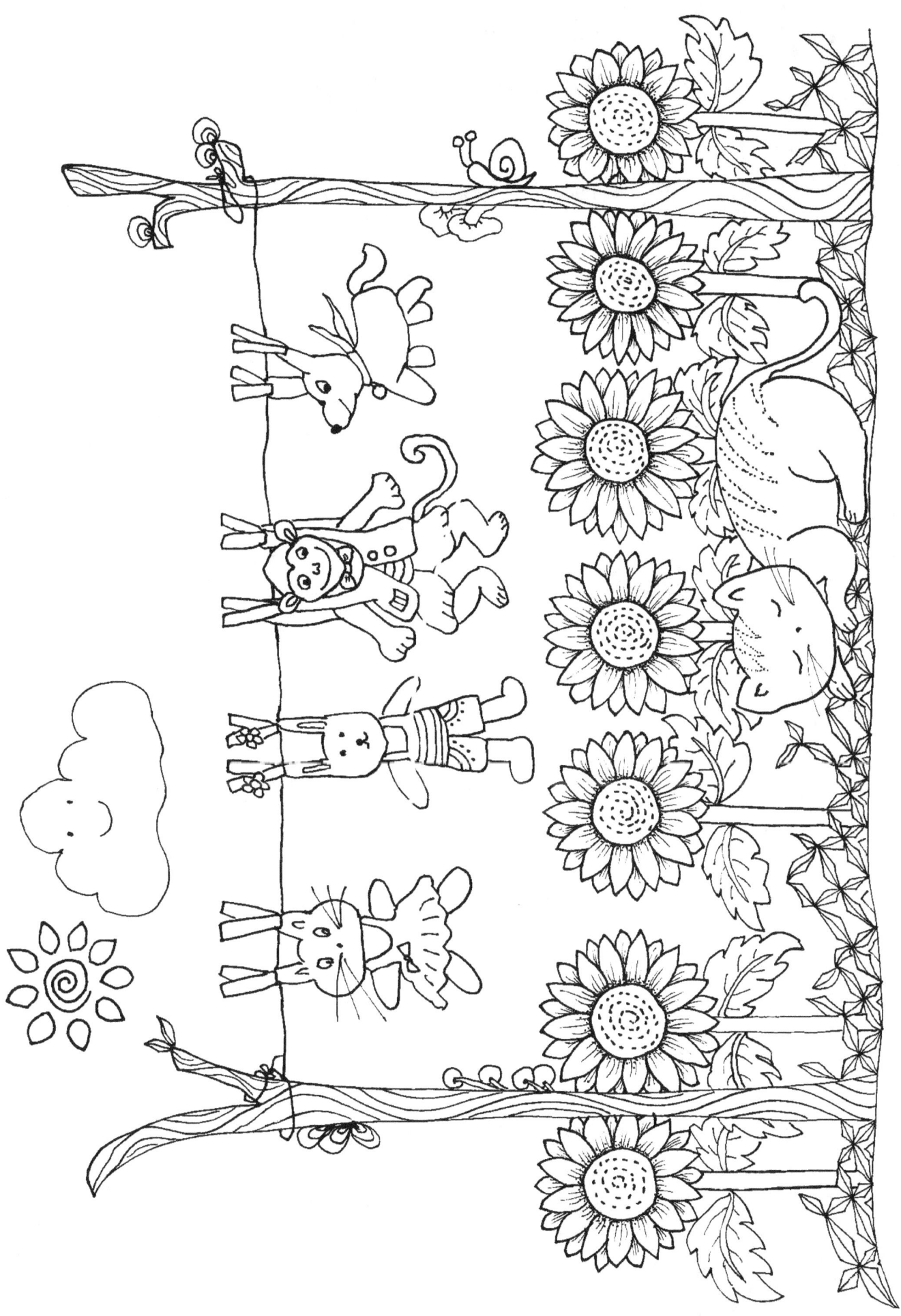

Contributing Artist
Jenny Wei
Taiwan

Facebook : zentanglefun

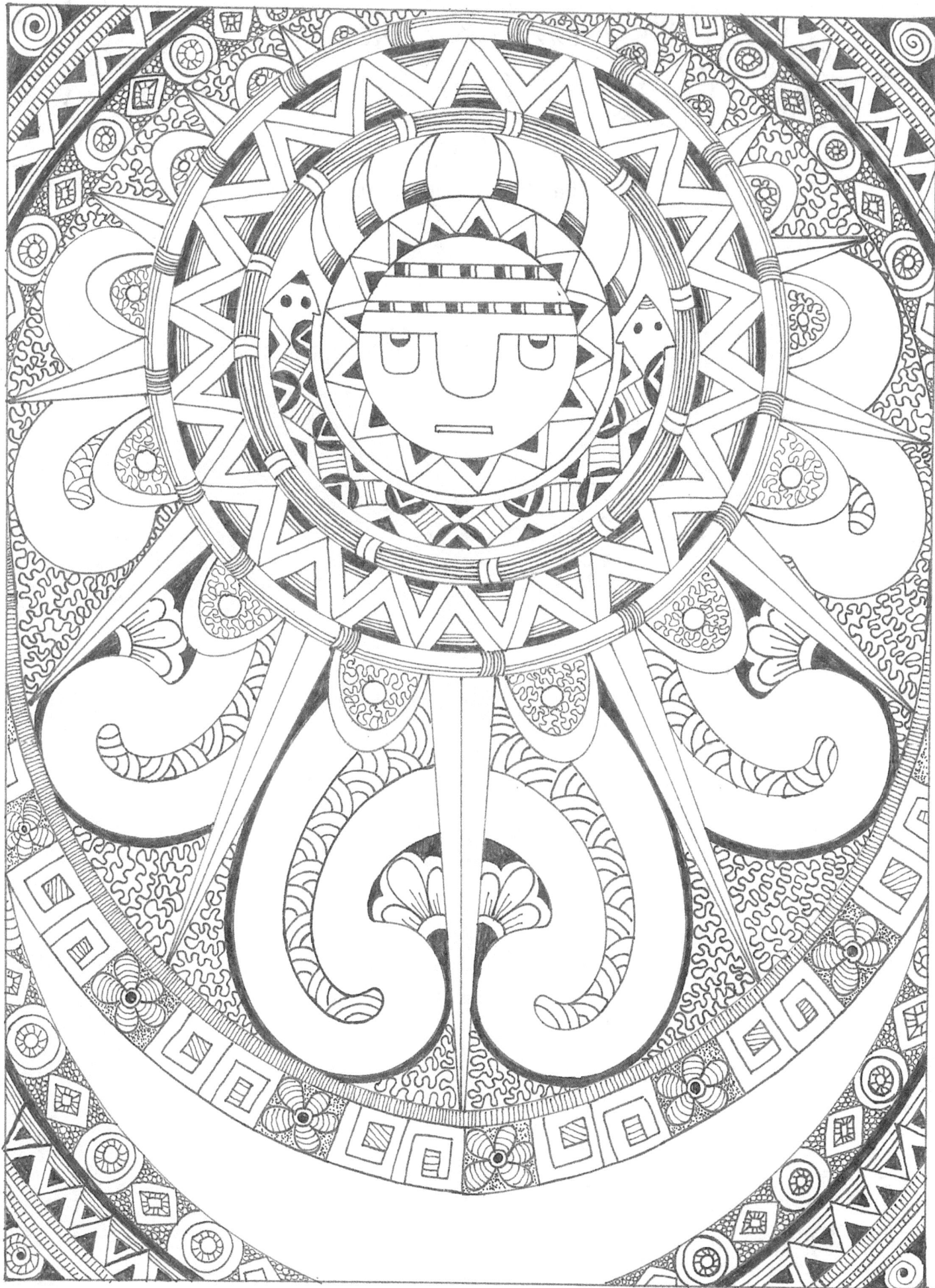

Contributing Artist
Jenny Wei
Taiwan

Facebook : zentanglefun

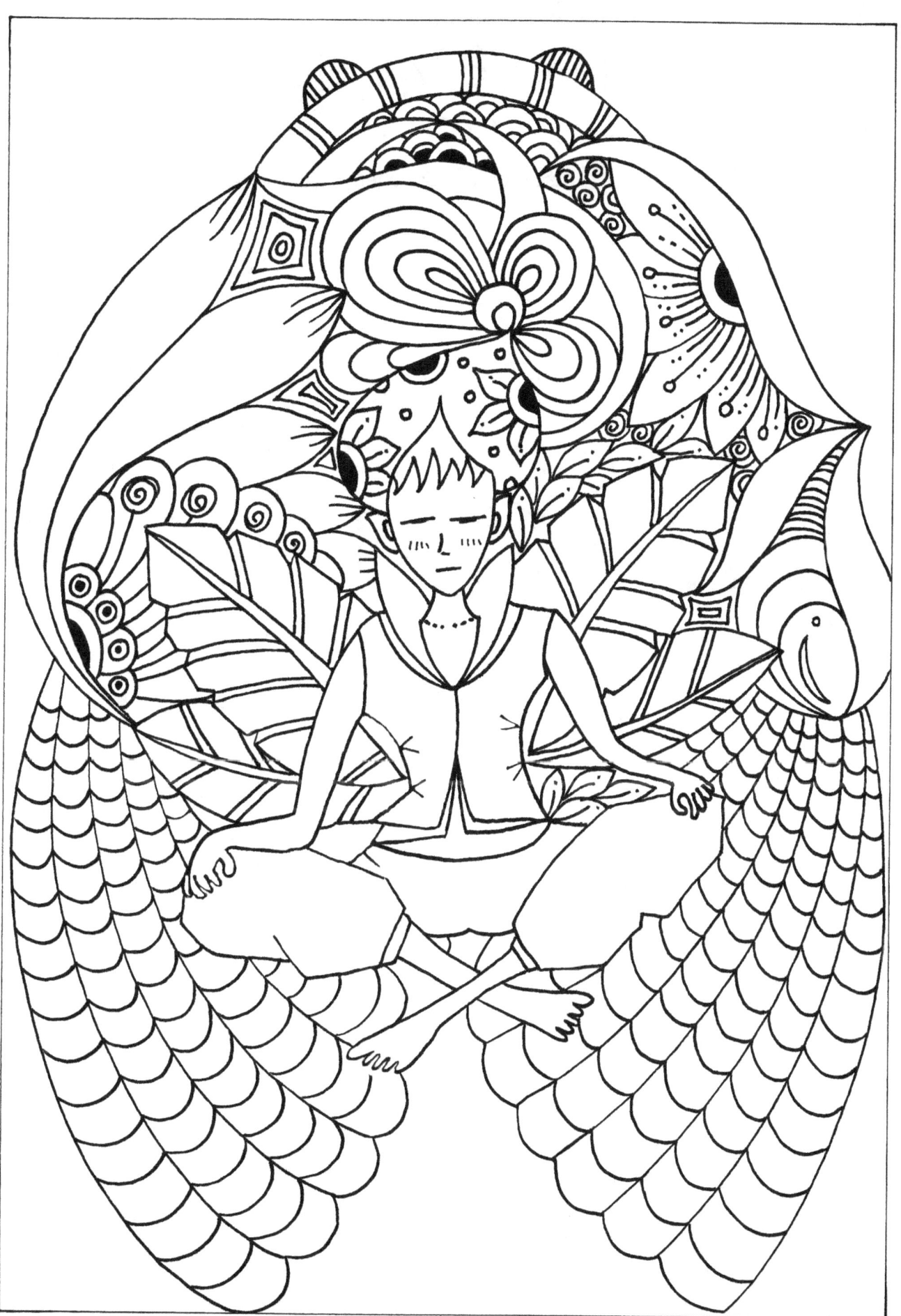

Contributing Artist
Pajun Chen
Taiwan

Facebook : pajunchen

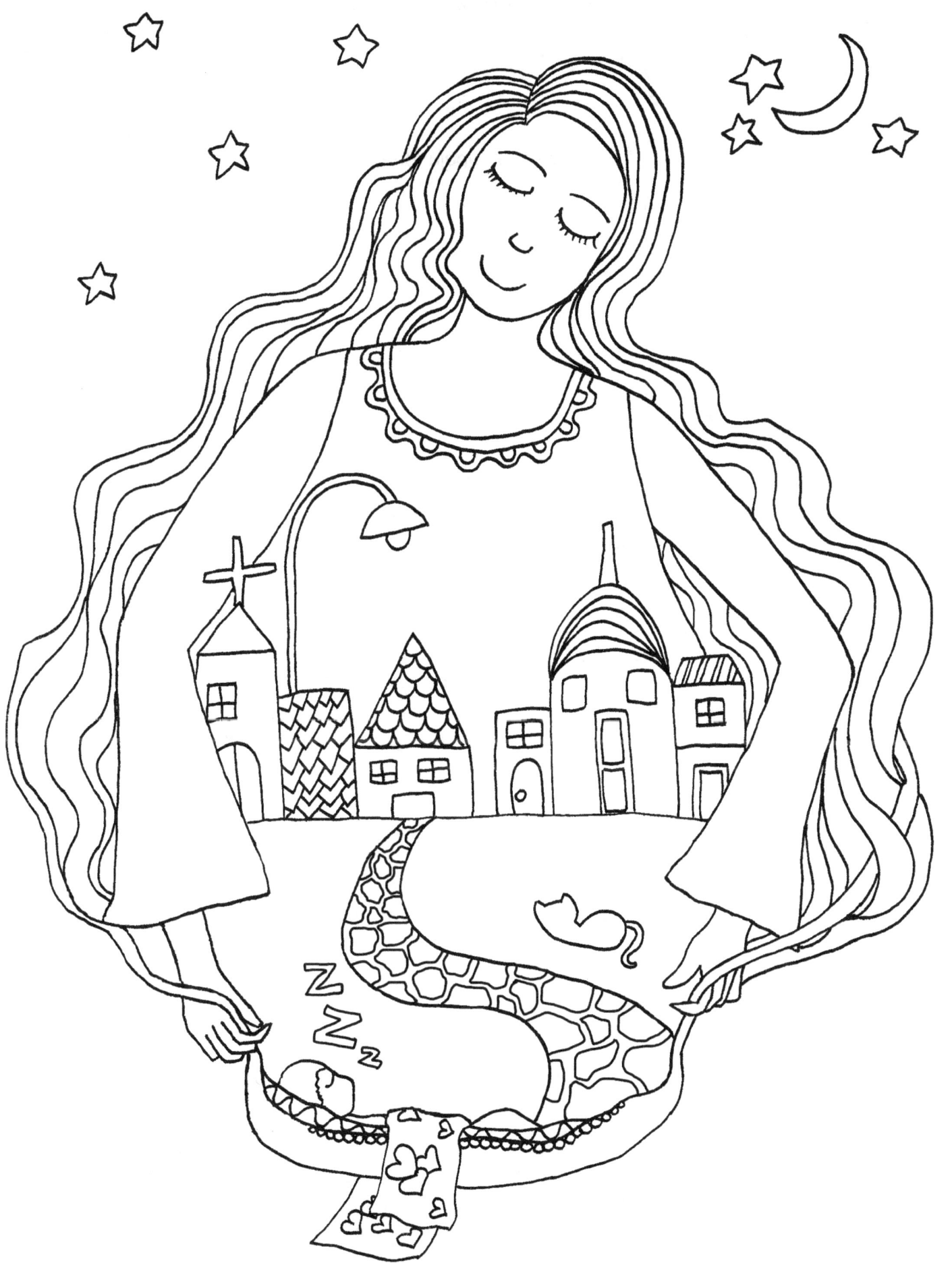

Contributing Artist
Pajun Chen
Taiwan

Facebook : pajunchen

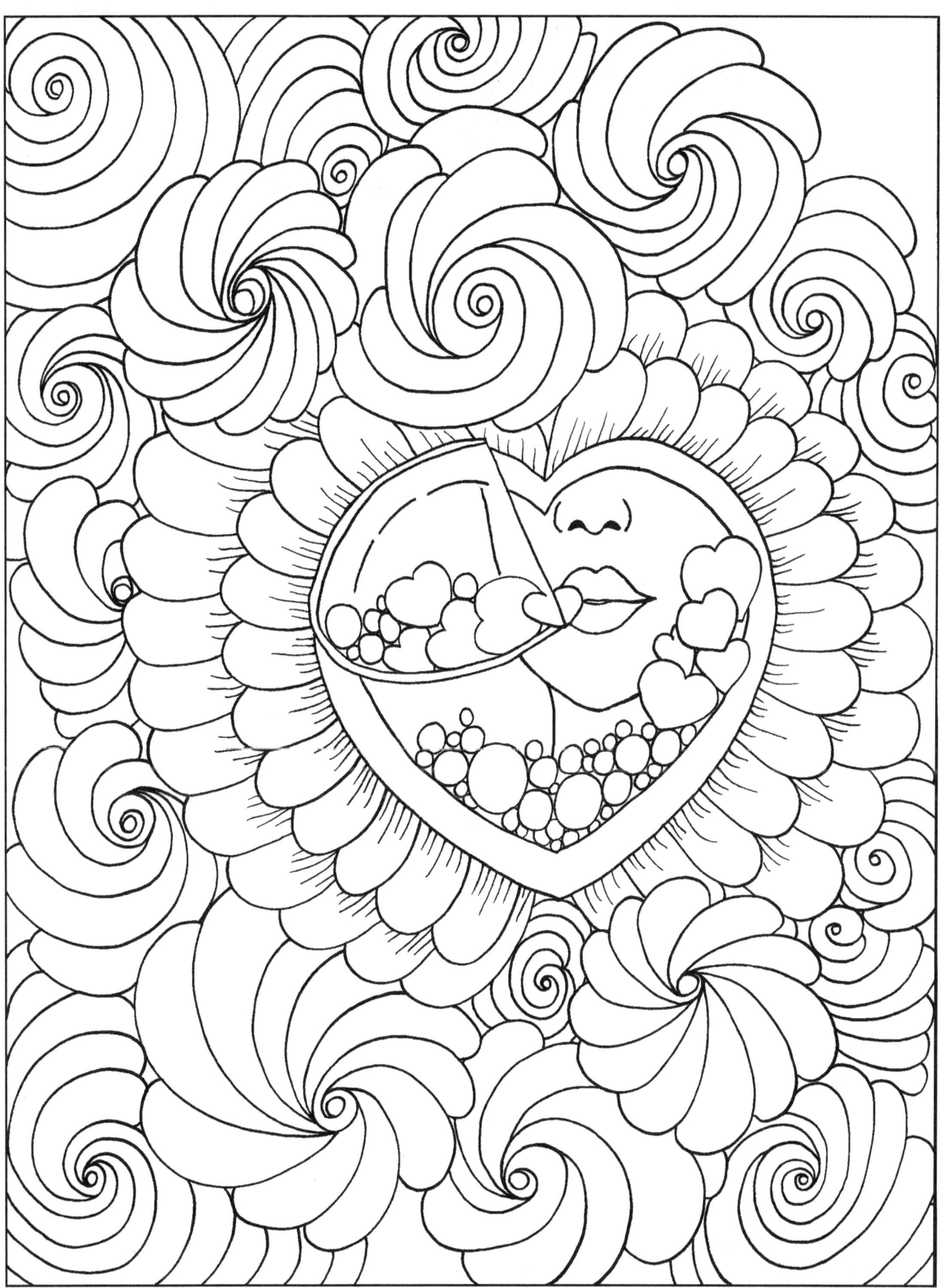

Contributing Artist
Wen Kung
Taiwan

https://www.facebook.com/Wen.Zentangle

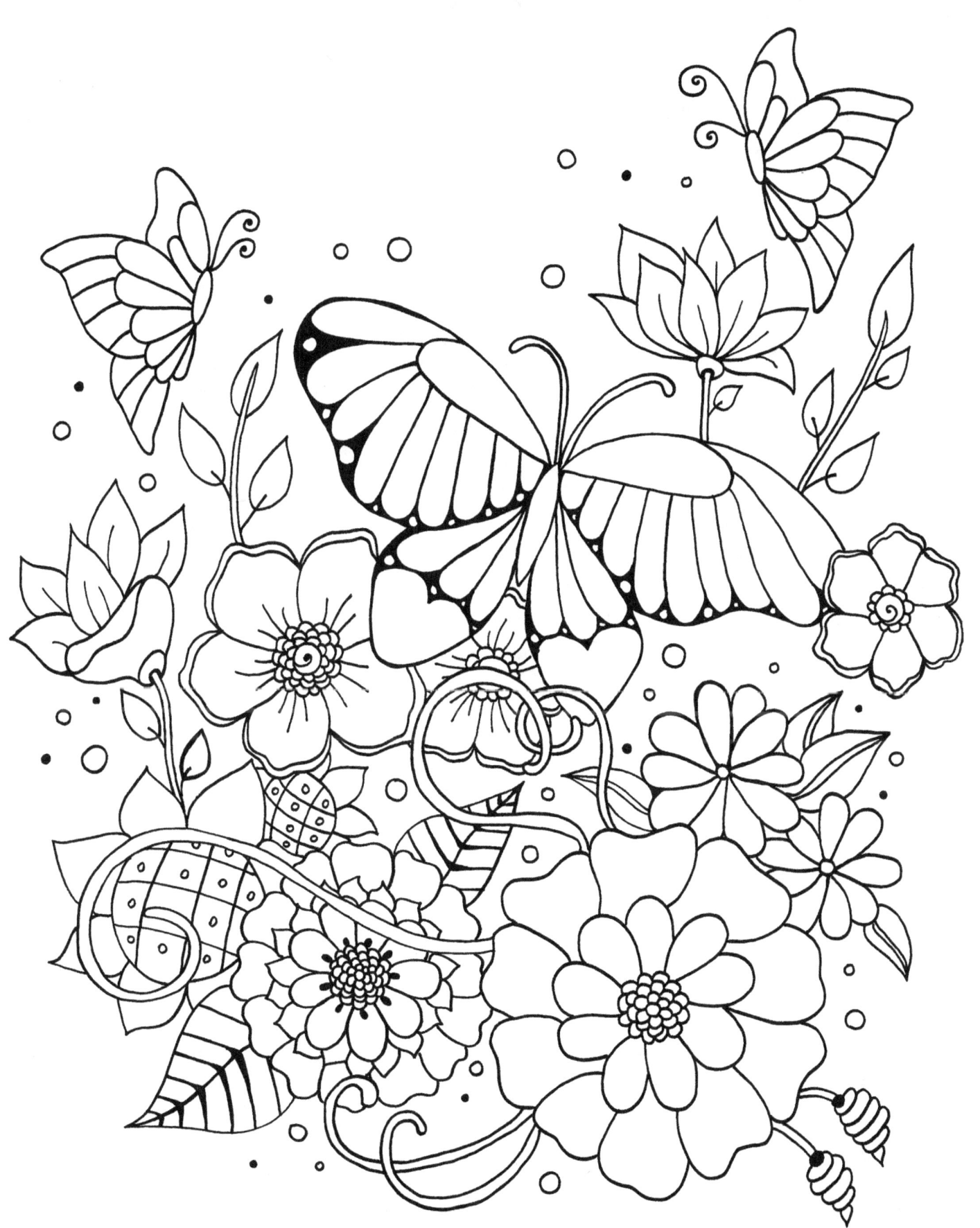

Contributing Artist
Wen Kung
Taiwan

https://www.facebook.com/Wen.Zentangle

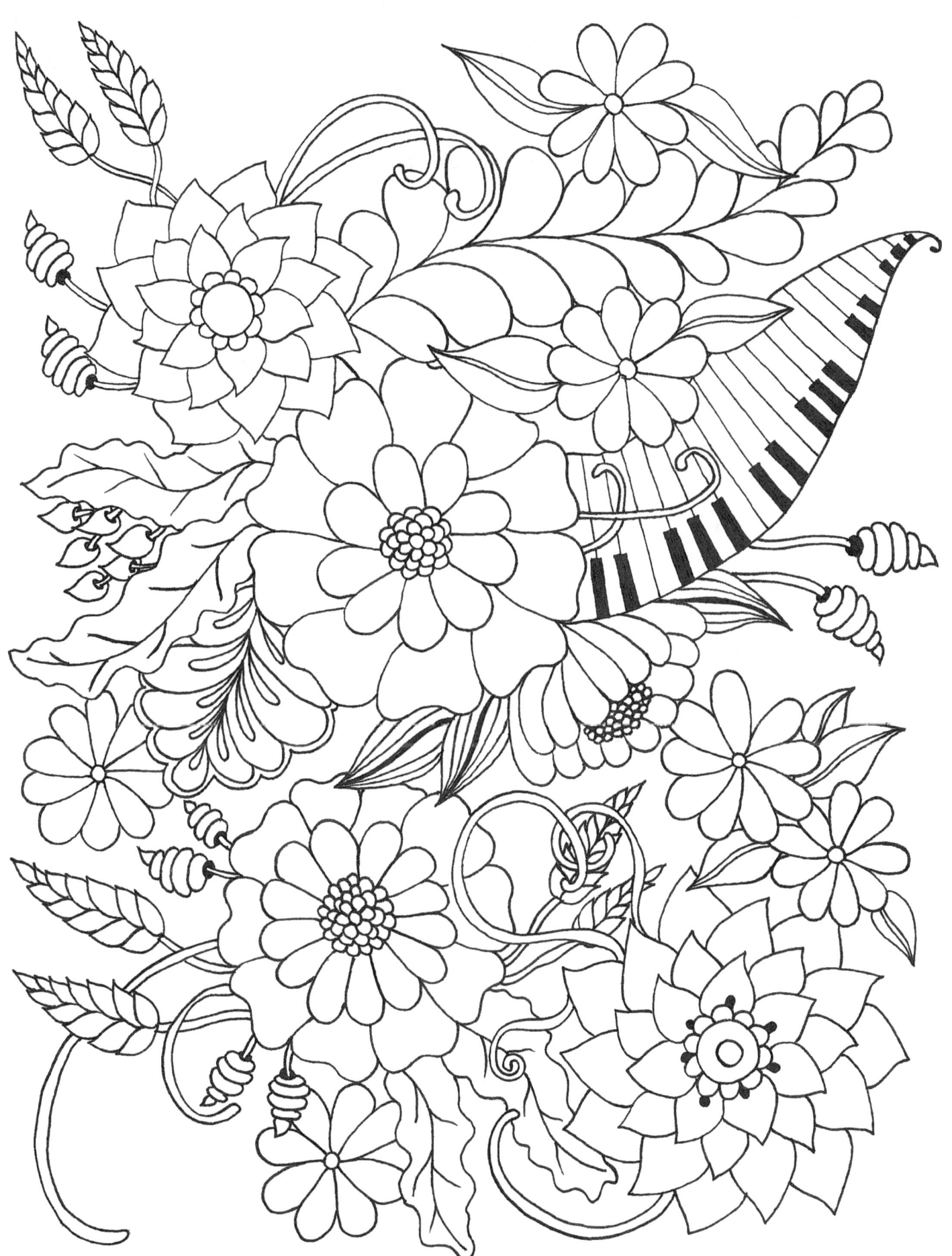

Contributing Artist
Hung Ai-Ling
Taiwan

Facebook : inspiredartLing

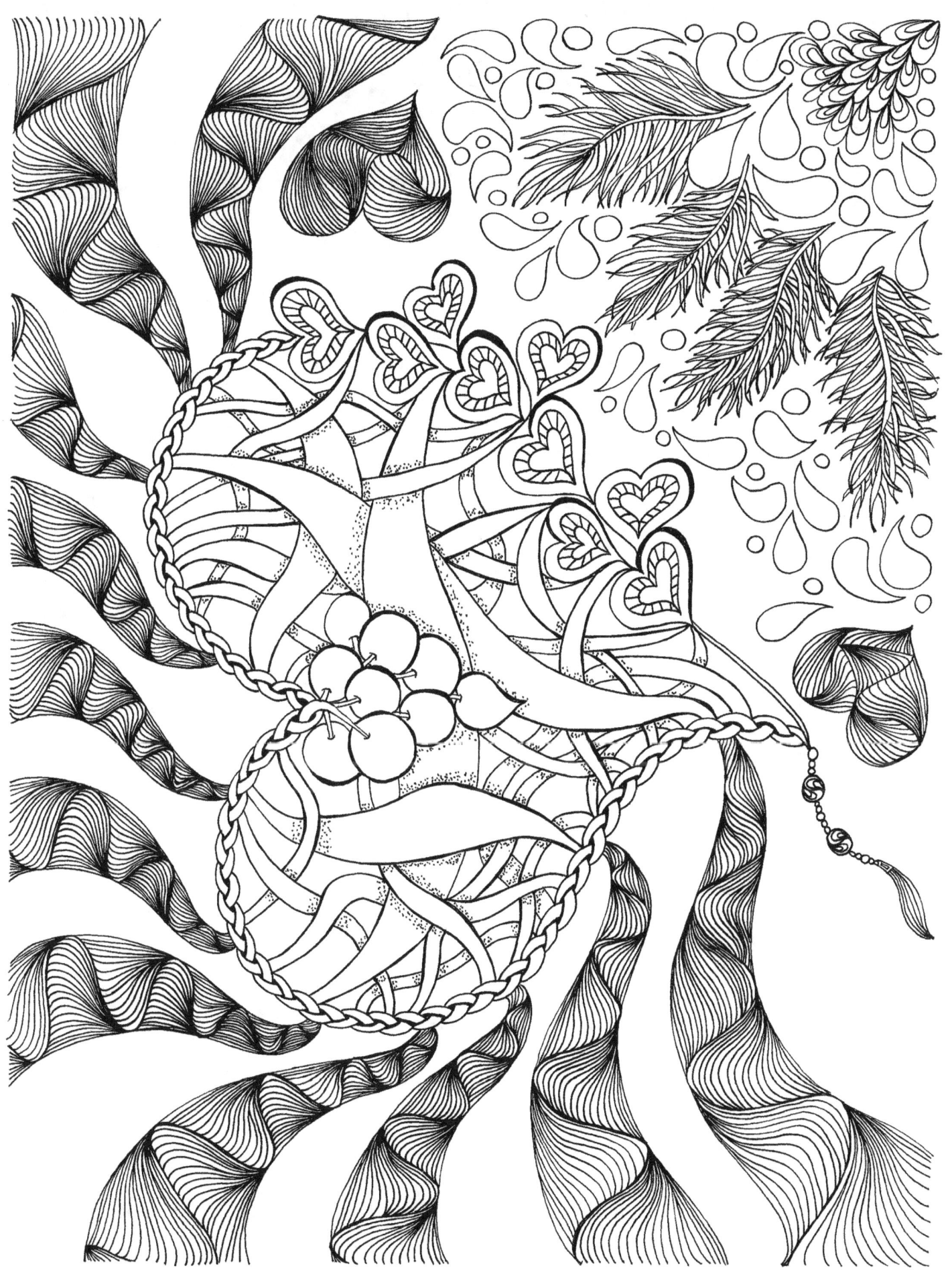

Contributing Artist
Hung Ai-Ling
Taiwan

Facebook : inspiredartLing

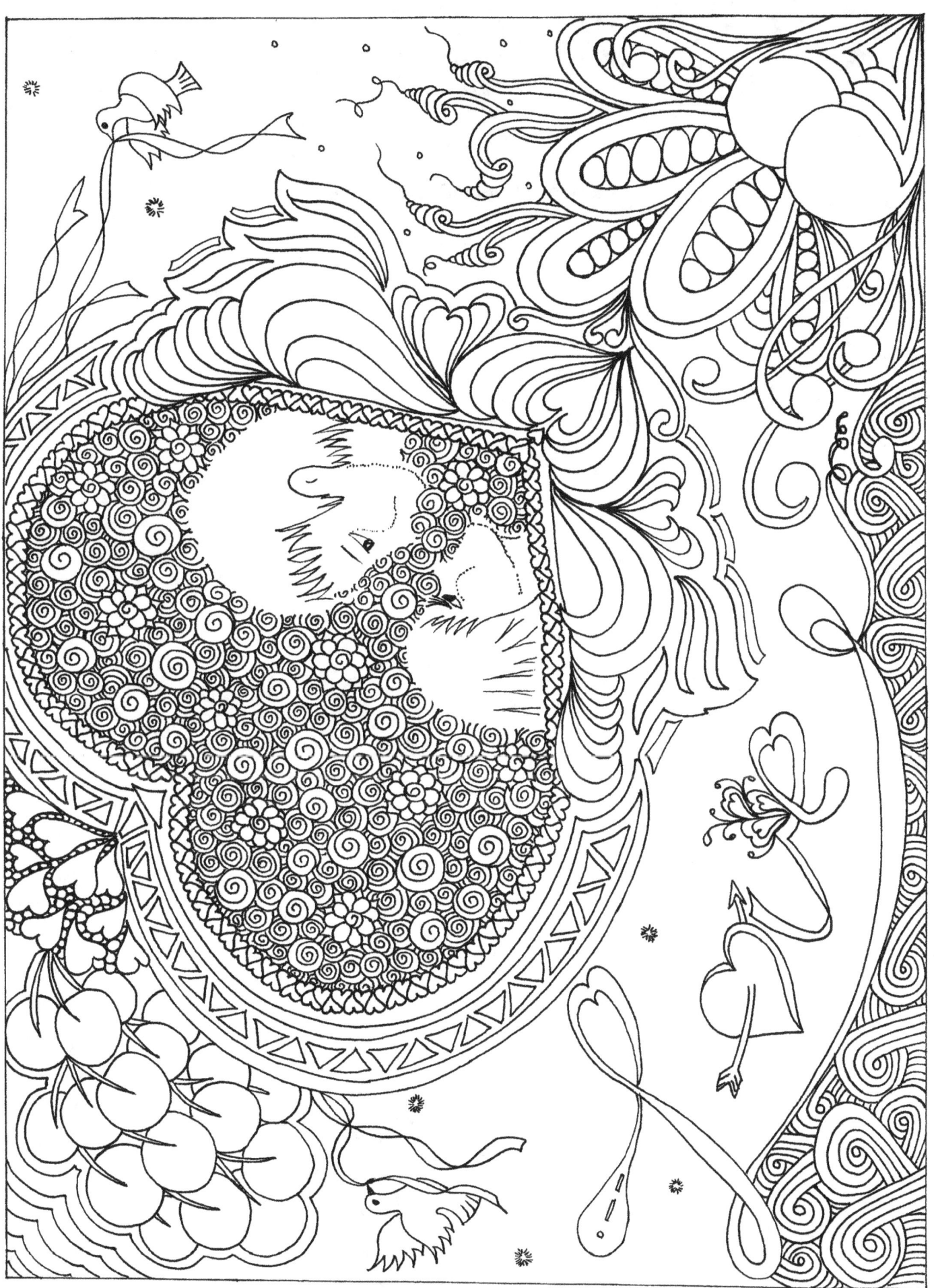

Contributing Artist
Debbie Lai
Taiwan

Facebook : DebbieDoodleGarden

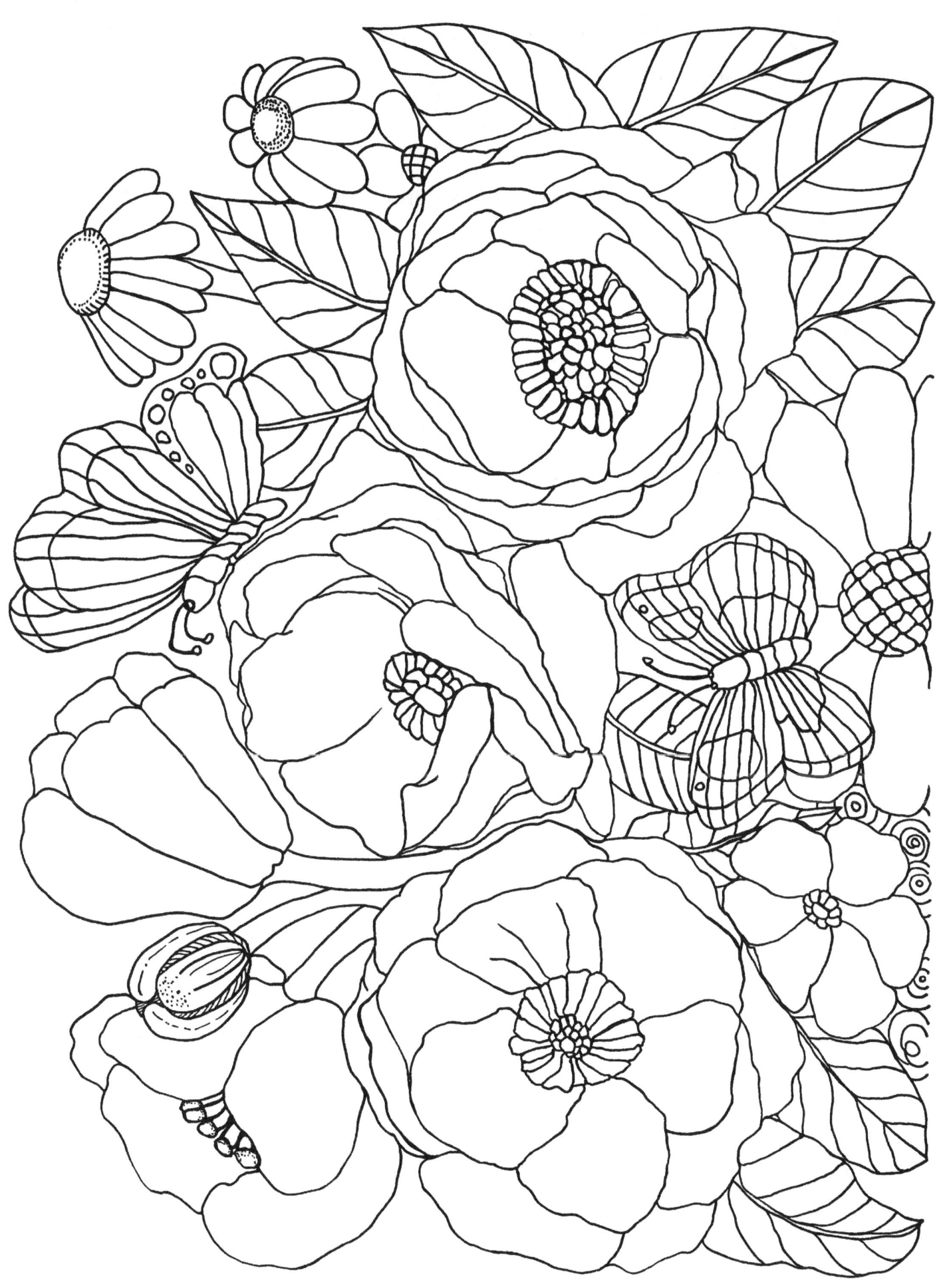

Contributing Artist
Debbie Lai
Taiwan

Facebook : DebbieDoodleGarden

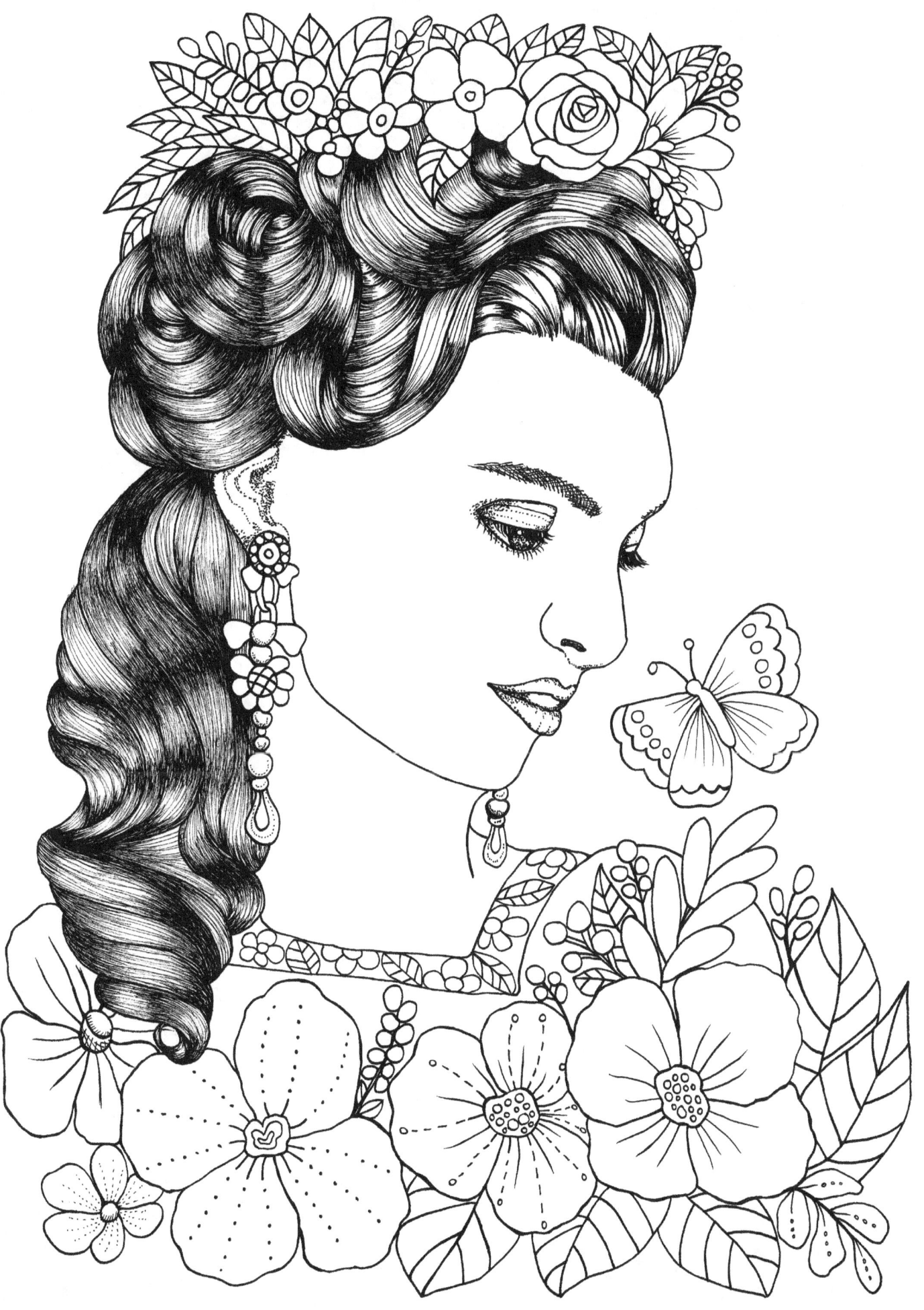

Contributing Artist
Mina Hsiao
Taiwan
https://www.facebook.com/czt19mina

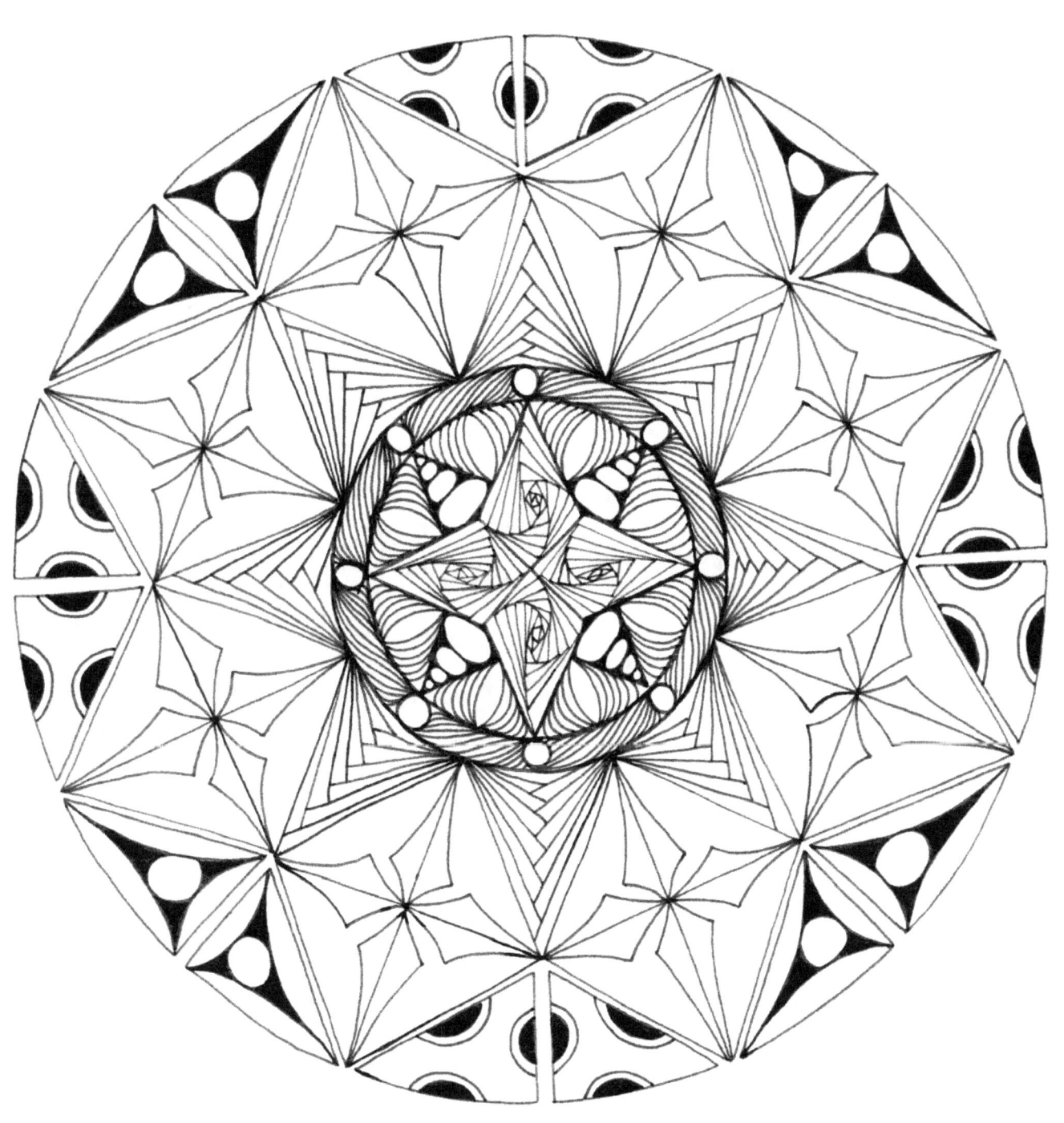

Contributing Artist
Mina Hsiao
Taiwan

https://www.facebook.com/czt19mina

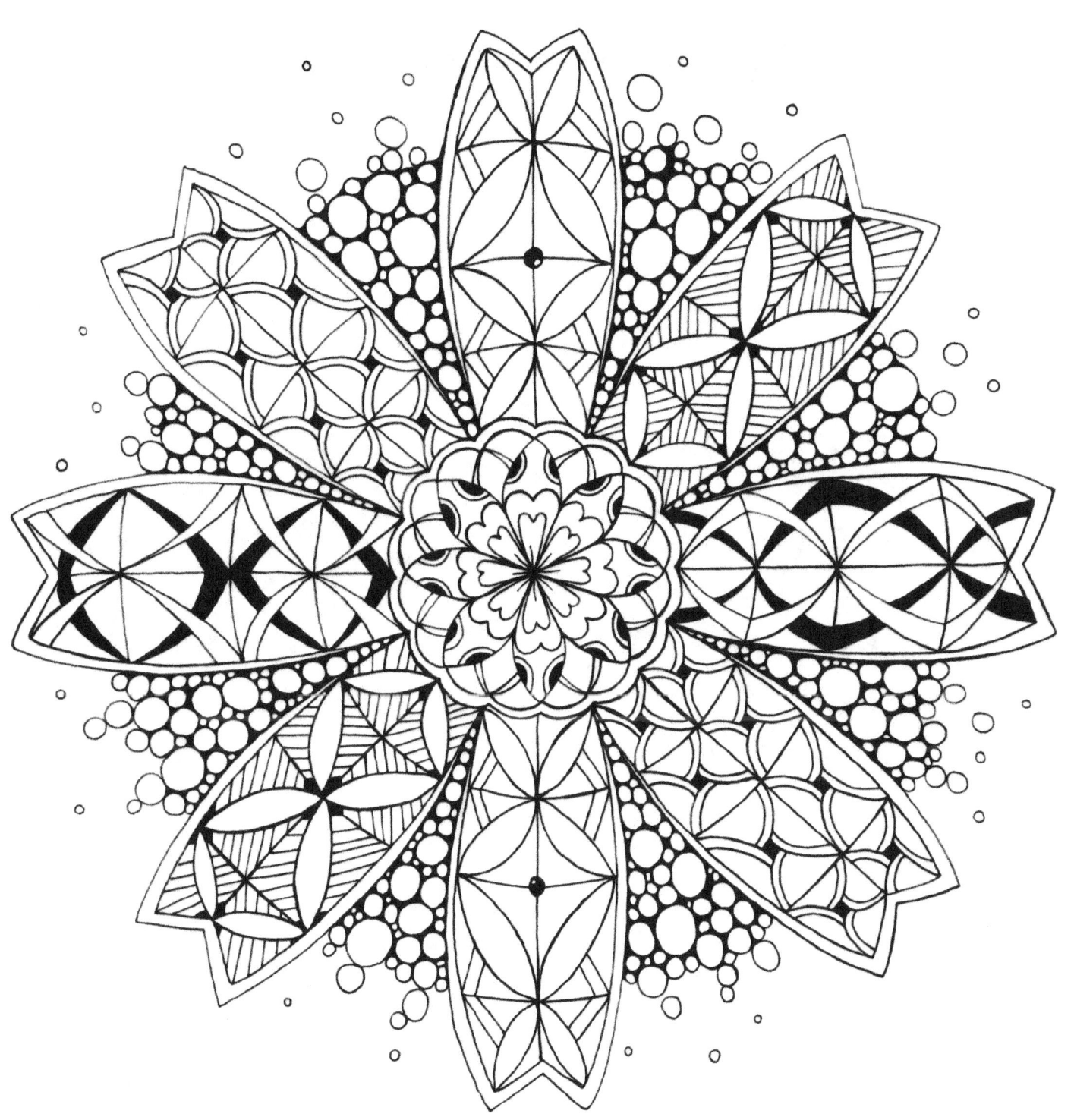

Contributing Artist
Alexius Hsing
Taiwan

Facebook : alexius.storry.teller

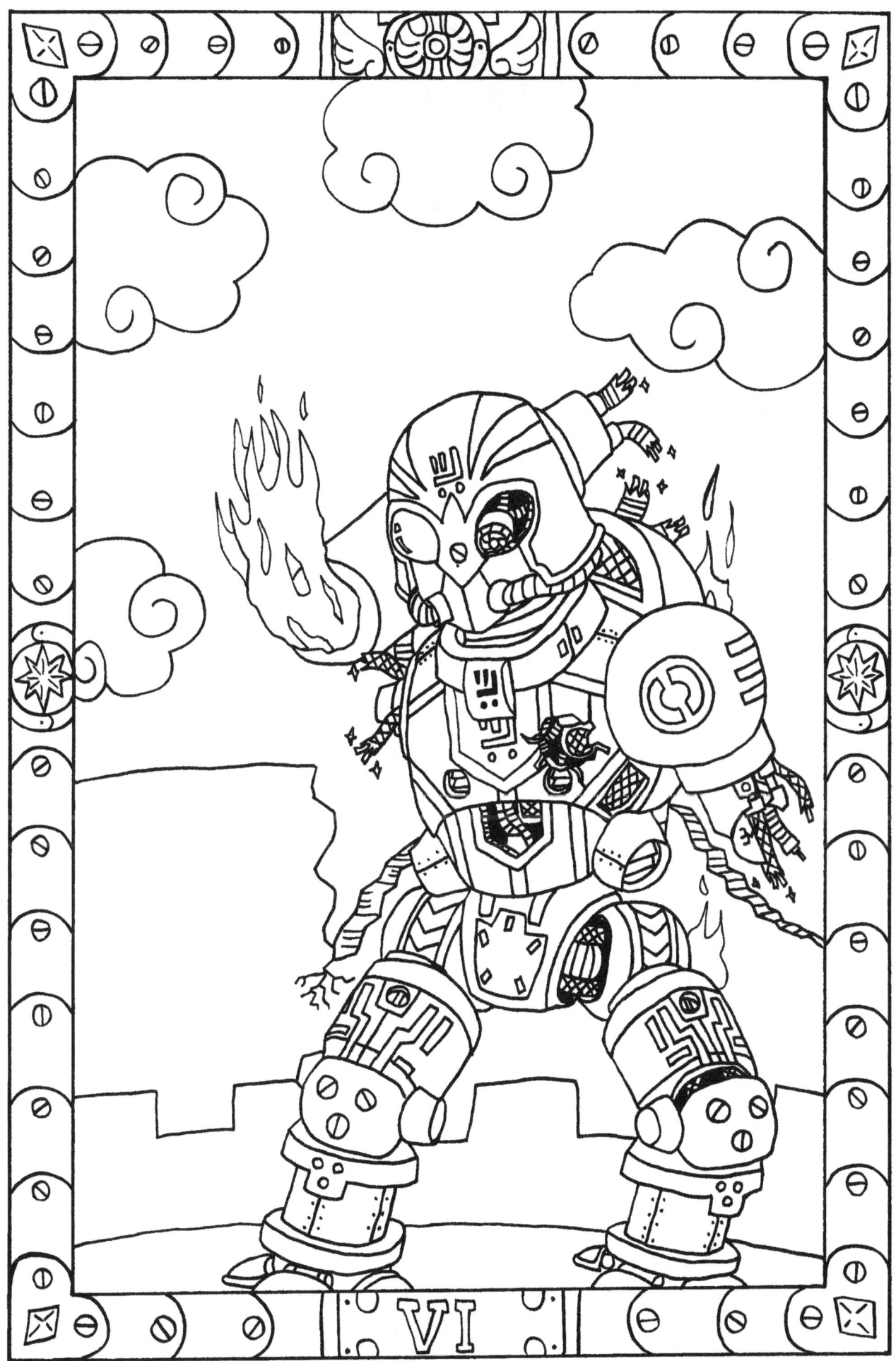

Contributing Artist
Alexius Hsing
Taiwan

Facebook : alexius.storry.teller

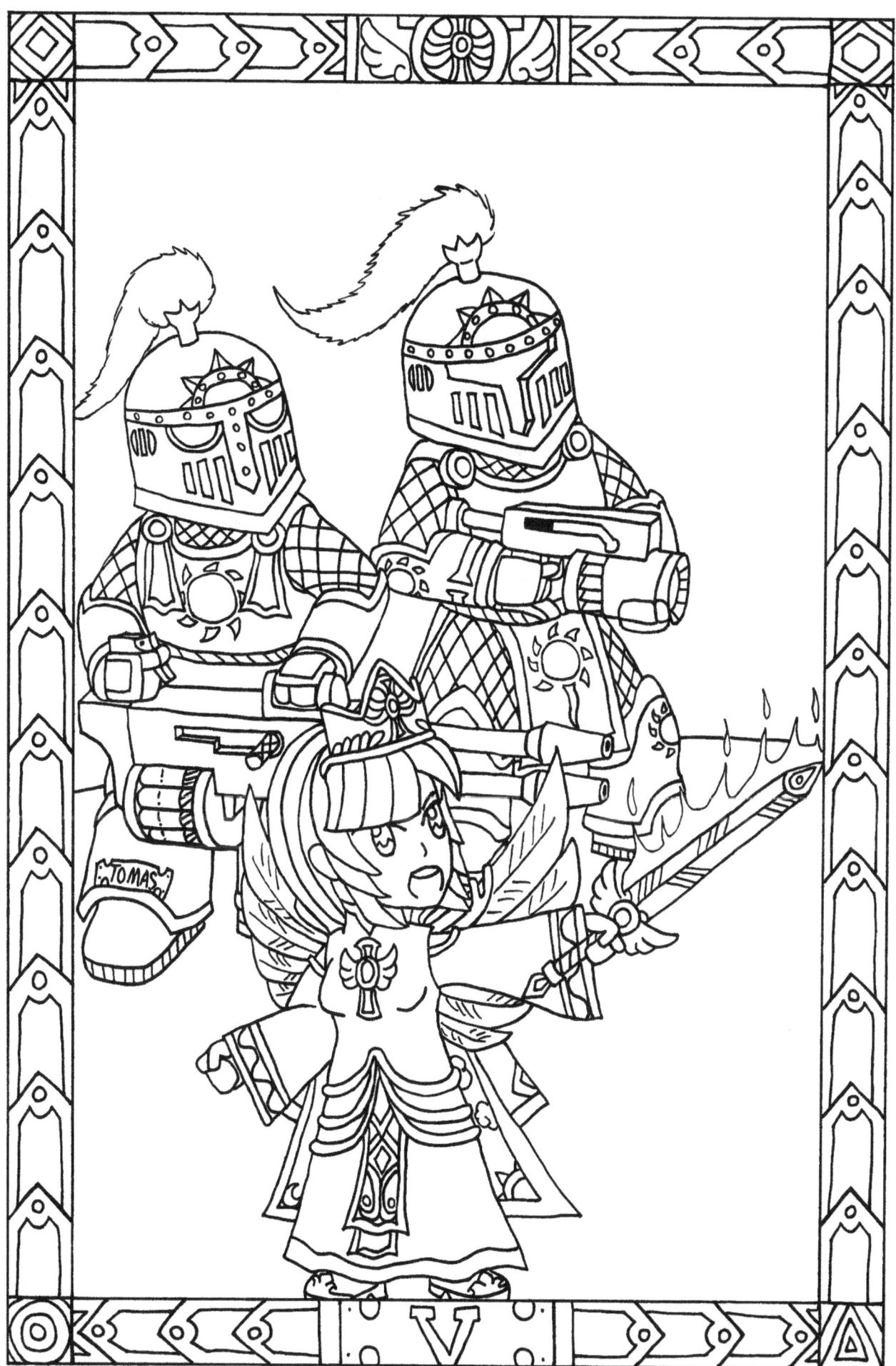

Contributing Artist
Jennifer Rainbow Beryllium
Taiwan

Facebook : DebbieDoodleGarden

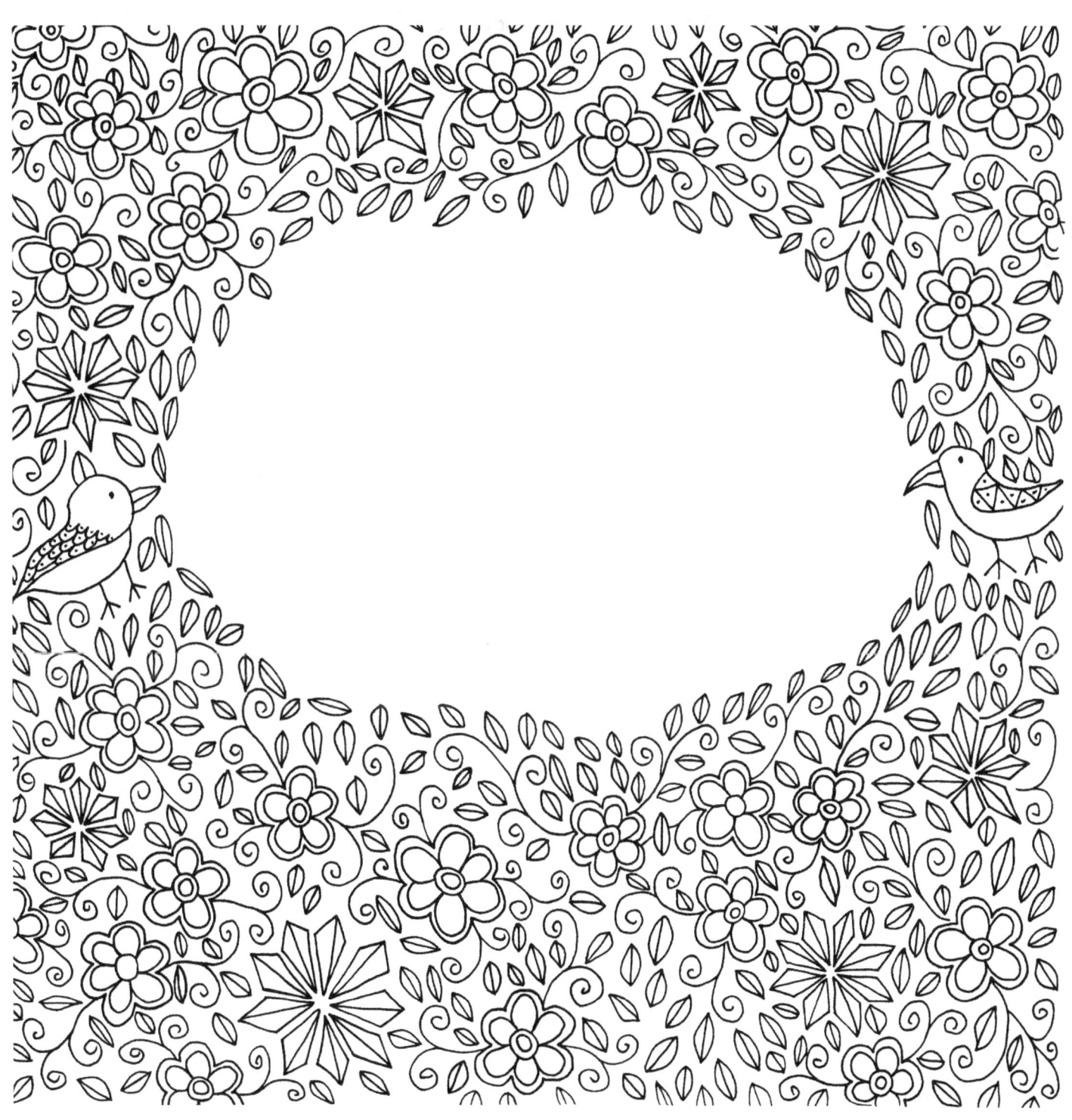

Contributing Artist
Jennifer Rainbow Beryllium
Taiwan

Facebook : DebbieDoodleGarden

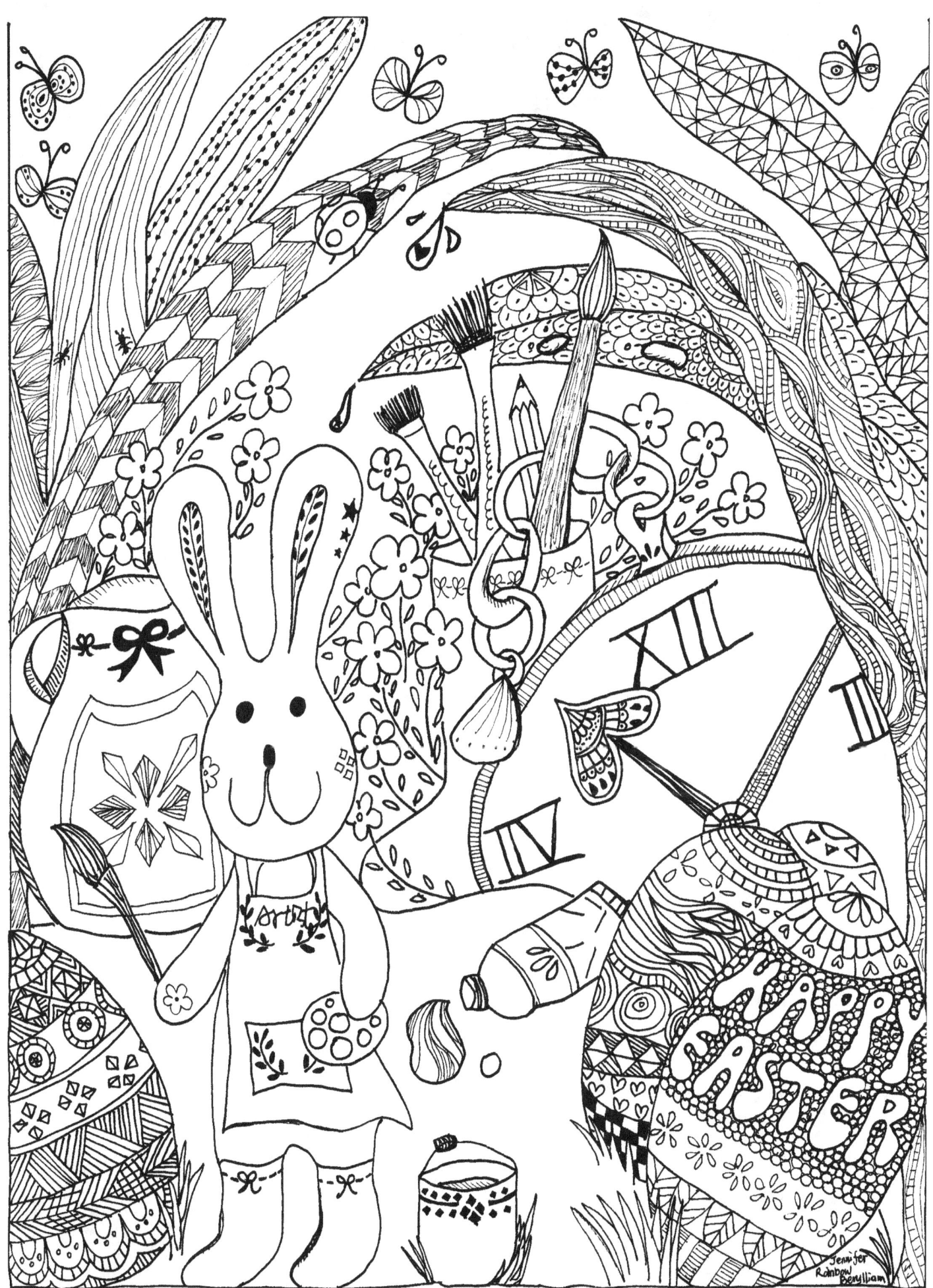

Contributing Artist
Kimiko Maeda
Taiwan

Facebook : kimikomaedahome

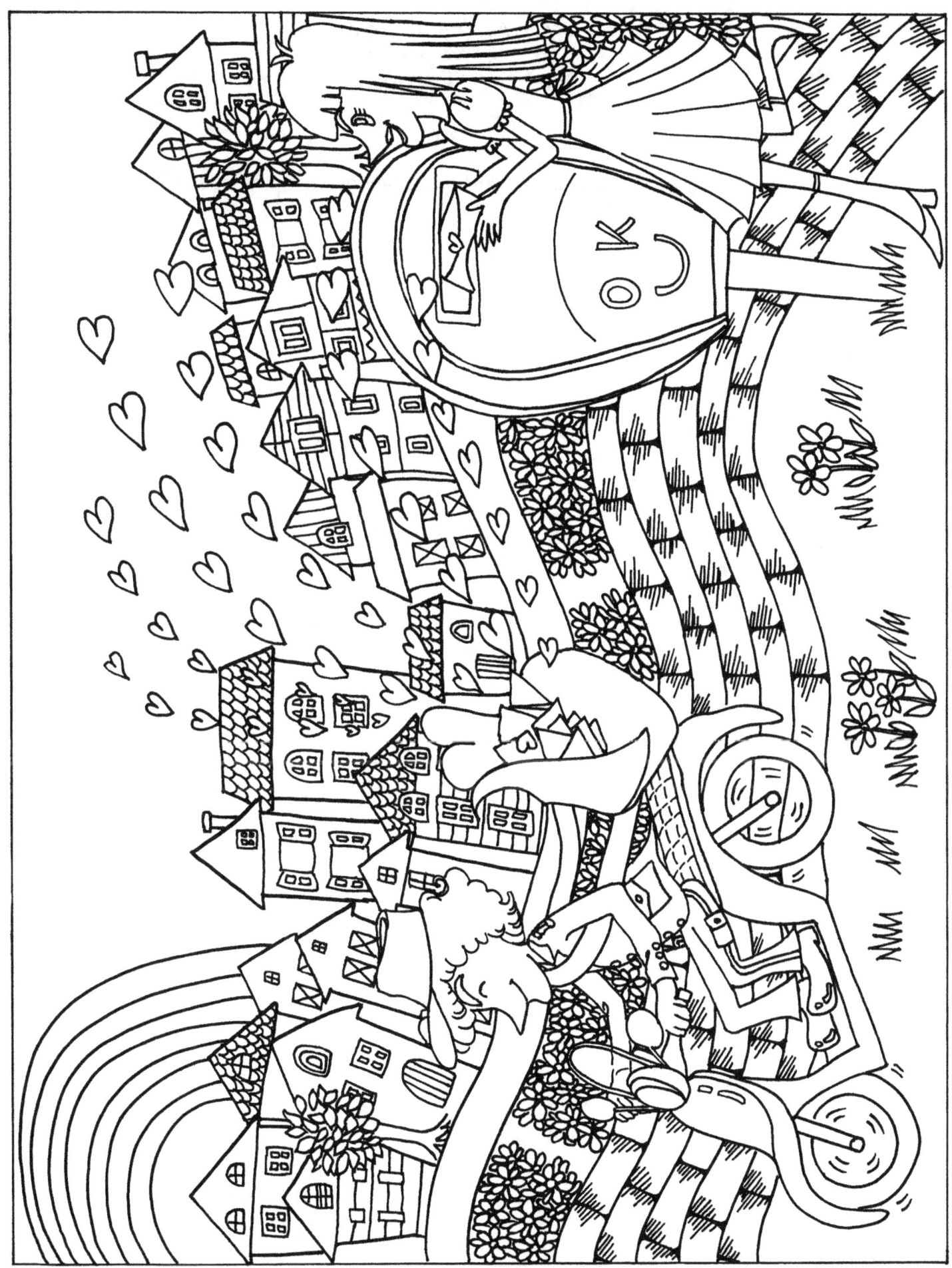

Contributing Artist
Kimiko Maeda
Taiwan

Facebook : kimikomaedahome

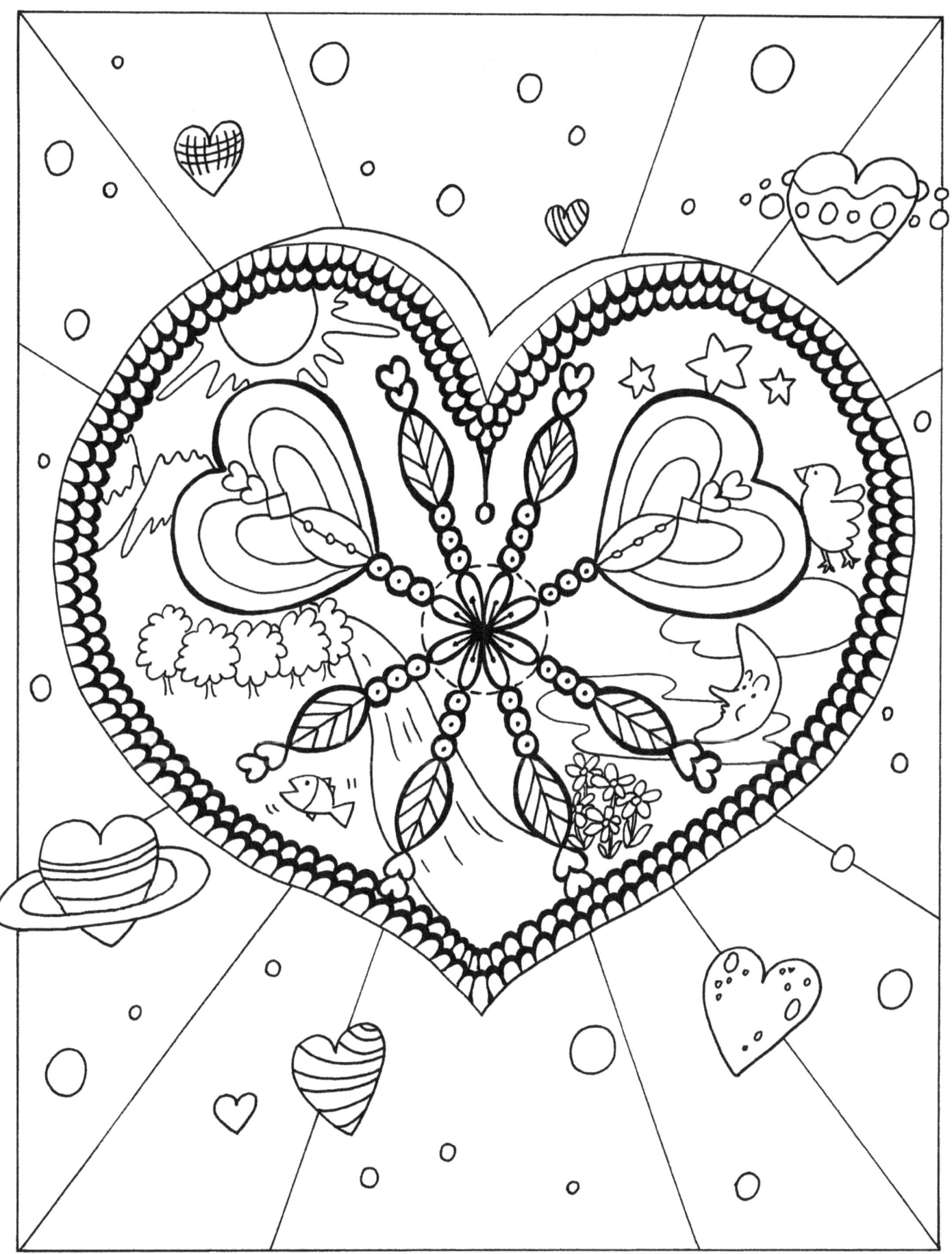

Contributing Artist
Jean Li
Taiwan

Facebook : JeanLi719

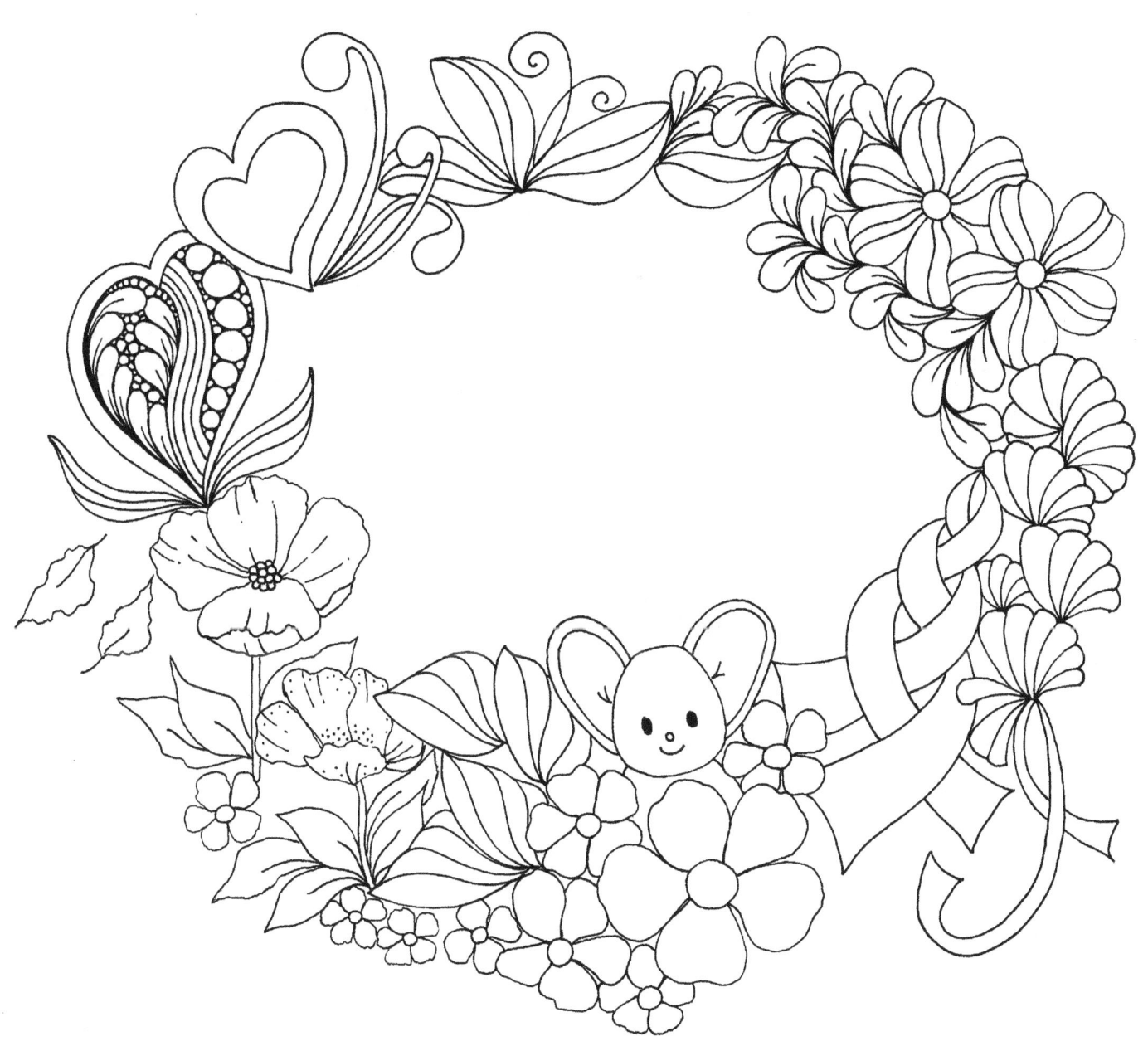

Contributing Artist
Jean Li
Taiwan

Facebook : JeanLi719

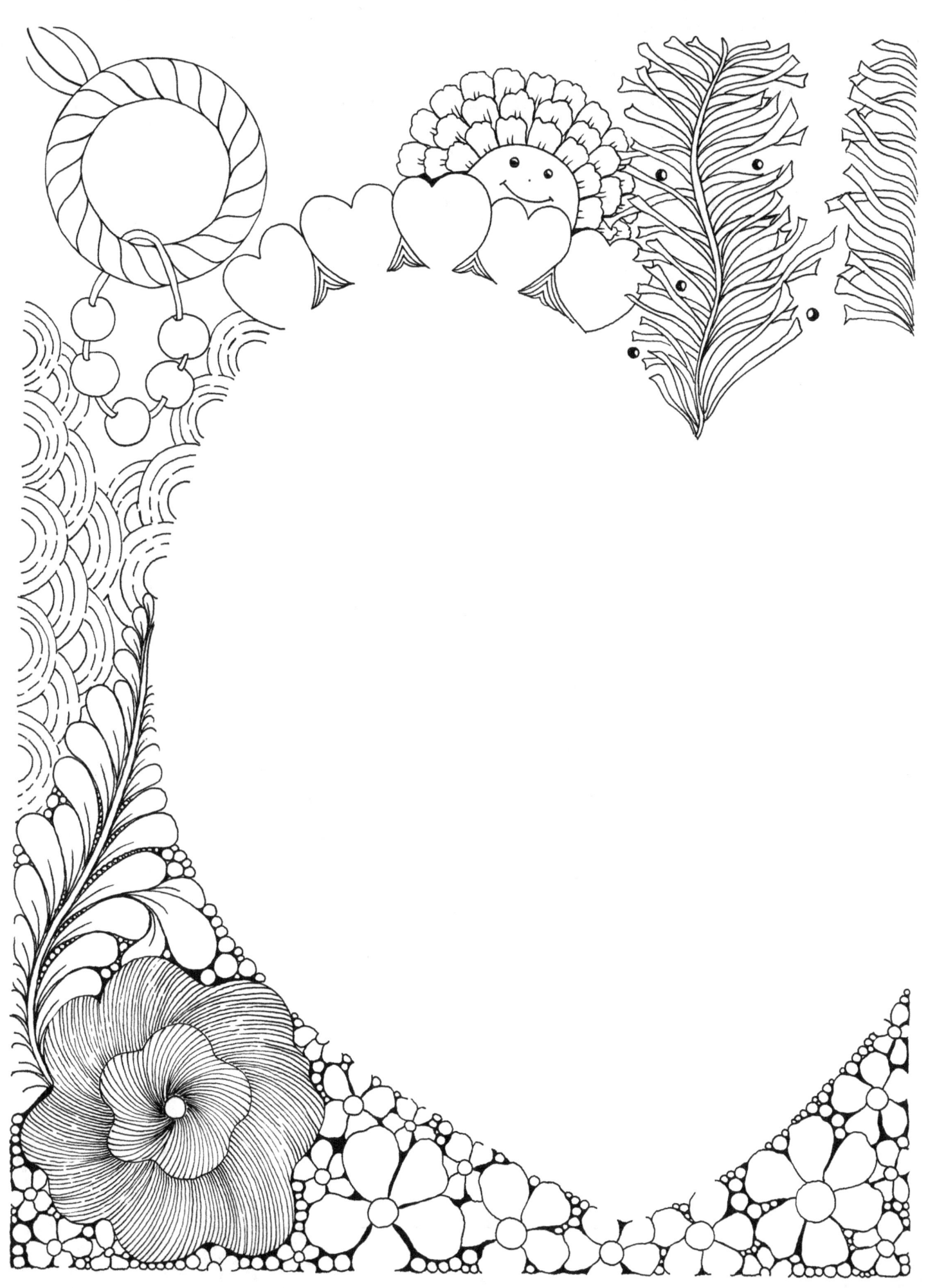

Test Your Colors here ....
Charts from "My Pocket Color Companion"
and
" My Color Companion"

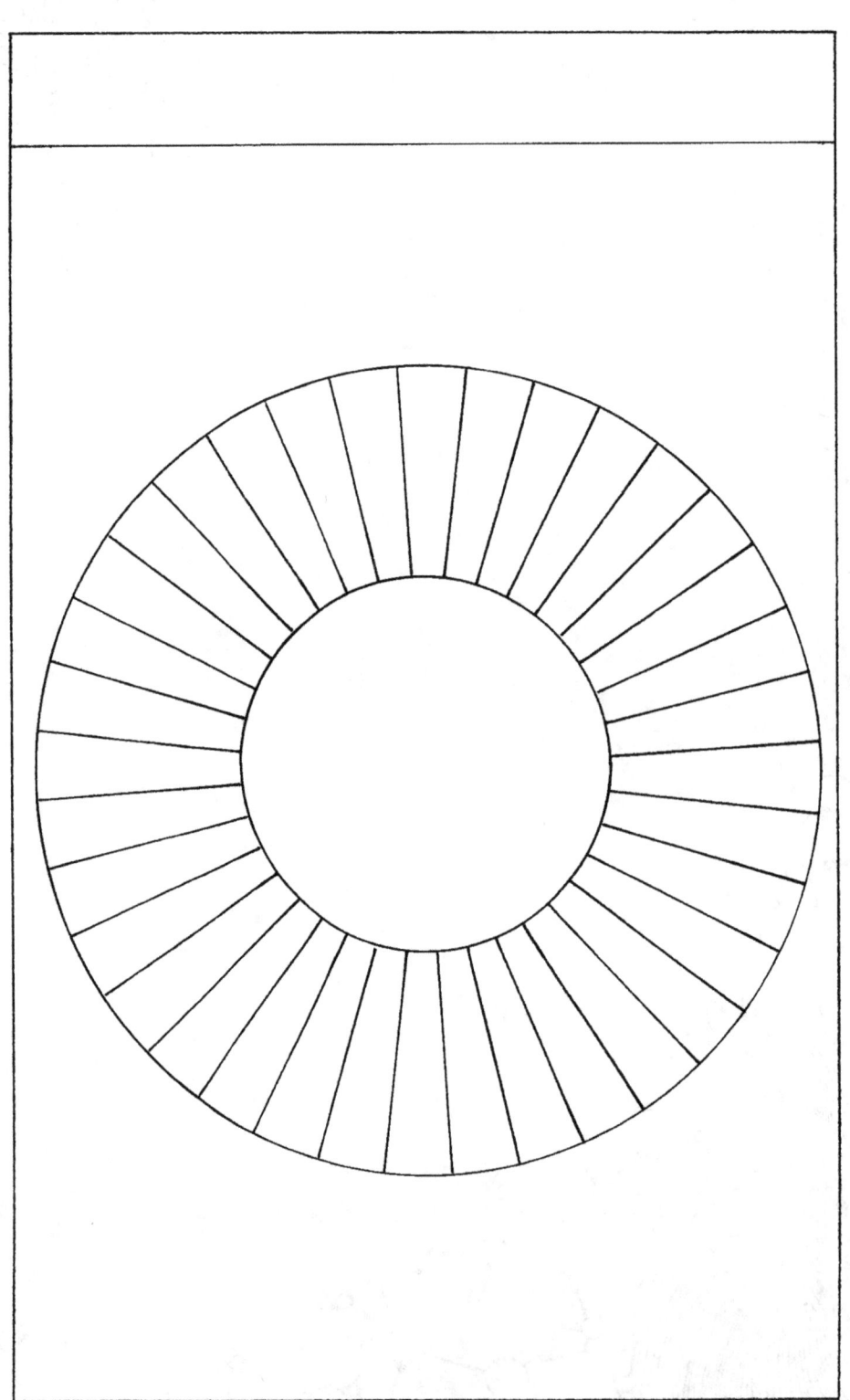

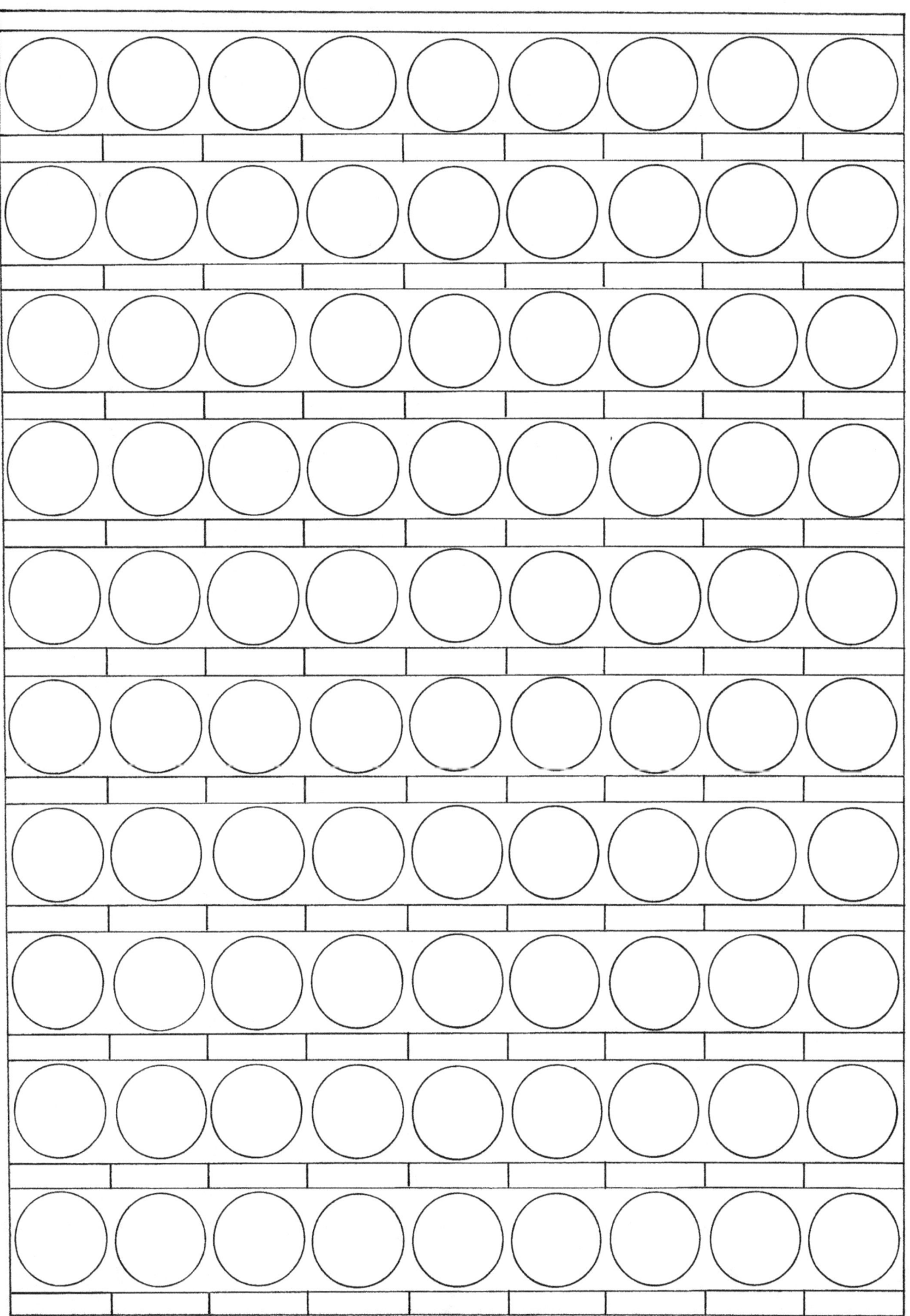

www.ingramcontent.com/pod-product-compliance
Lightning Source LLC
Chambersburg PA
CBHW082338220526
45470CB00008B/2550